Our Non-Christian Nation

OUR NON-CHRISTIAN NATION

*How Atheists, Satanists, Pagans,
and Others Are Demanding
Their Rightful Place in Public Life*

JAY WEXLER

REDWOOD PRESS
Stanford, California

STANFORD UNIVERSITY PRESS

Stanford, California

Printed in the United States of America on acid-free, archival-quality paper

Library of Congress Cataloging-in-Publication Data

Names: Wexler, Jay.

Title: Our non-Christian nation : how atheists, Satanists, pagans, and others are demanding their rightful place in public life / Jay Wexler.

Description: Stanford, California : Stanford University Press, 2019. | Includes bibliographical references and index.

Identifiers: LCCN 2018040467 (print) | LCCN 2018044465 (ebook) | ISBN 9780804798990 (cloth : alk. paper) | ISBN 9781503609068 (ebook)

Subjects: LCSH: Religious minorities—Civil rights—United States—Cases. | Religious law and legislation—United States—Cases. | Freedom of speech—United States—Cases. | United States. Supreme Court—History. | Religious pluralism—United States. | Religion and state—United States.

Classification: LCC KF4755 (ebook) | LCC KF4755 .W49 2019 (print) | DDC 342.7308/52—dc23

LC record available athttps://lccn.loc.gov/2018040467

Cover design: Christian Fuenfhausen

Text design: Kevin Barrett Kane

Typeset at Stanford University Press in 10/15 Sabon

For all the courageous plaintiffs who have fought
for the separation of church and state

Contents

Our Non-Christian Nation

INTRODUCTION

THE RESIDENTS of Belle Plaine, Minnesota, would probably like the world to think that the town's population is 6,600 or 6,700, but according to the 2010 census (and as reported on the highway signs that mark the town borders), its actual population is 6,661. With a number like that, could it really be just a coincidence that this homey, homogeneous hamlet about forty minutes southwest of Minneapolis would have instigated a nationwide controversy over the First Amendment when it became the first city ever to authorize the erection of a Satanic monument on government property?

Yes. Yes, of course it's a coincidence. But kind of a funny one, you have to admit, right?

It all started when the family of a veteran named Joe installed a small monument in Joe's honor on the grounds of the peaceful Veterans Memorial Park a few blocks from what counts as downtown Belle Plaine. The monument is a black silhouette of a soldier kneeling before a cross. The whole thing is maybe two feet wide by two feet high, and if it hadn't been for a resident of the town who had been harassed for her non-Christian beliefs in the past, the monument (which is widely known simply as "Joe") would probably have gone unnoticed by anyone outside the town.

This resident, however, was offended that the town had placed a cross on public property, so in August 2016 she contacted the Freedom from Religion

Foundation (FFRF), an Atheist activist group working out of Madison, Wisconsin, that over the years has aggressively brought legal actions to enforce its strict view of the separation of church and state. FFRF threatened the city with a lawsuit if it didn't remove the cross from the monument, so the town—its coffers not exactly overflowing with cash for defending itself in federal court—ordered in January 2017 that the cross be removed.

Residents of the town—almost all of them white Christians—rebelled. Citizens gathered daily at the park holding flags and crosses. Many put two-dimensional cutout versions of Joe on the outsides of their homes to show support for the Christian monument. At a heated city council meeting in early February, more than a hundred citizens stood shoulder to shoulder, filling the cramped chambers of the city hall on Meridian Street to ask the council to revisit its decision. Referring to FFRF as a "cowardly out-of-state hate group," a speaker representing the town's veterans called for the council to create a "free speech zone" or "limited public forum" within the park where private parties, including Joe's family, could erect monuments to honor the town's veterans.

After some debate and reworking of the original proposal, the city council in February adopted a resolution creating an area inside the park measuring seven feet by three and a half feet for such displays. These memorials would be approved on a first-come, first-served basis without respect to their religious content and could remain in the zone for up to one year. Signs posted near the forum would explain that the displays within the zone were the expressions of private individuals and were not being endorsed by the city. Very soon after the creation of the free speech zone, Joe's family returned the black silhouette monument in its original form, complete with the cross, to Veterans Memorial Park.

Creation of the free speech zone seemed to be enough to satisfy FFRF, but it also provided a new opportunity for a religious group headquartered in Salem, Massachusetts, known as the Satanic Temple. TST, as it's often called, was founded by a group of Satanists a few years back and quickly gained a national reputation for some of its high-visibility activities, including its July 2013 "Pink Mass," at which a bunch of gay and lesbian couples made out at the Meridian, Mississippi, gravesite of the mother of Fred Phelps, the leader of the horrific anti-gay hate group known as the Westboro Baptist Church. I will have a lot to say about TST later in the book, but for now the key thing to know about it is that one of its primary projects as an organization is to demand that the government treat all religions equally. In other words, if a city or town or state puts up a Christian monument on public property, then TST will insist that it put up a Satanic monument as well.

The Satanic Temple applied for permission to place a Satanic monument in the free speech zone at Veterans Memorial Park, and the city council, following the terms of its resolution, agreed, thus making Belle Plaine the first town in the United States to grant approval for a Satanic monument to be erected on public property. Perhaps the town thought it was just calling the Satanists' bluff, but if that was the case, it severely underestimated TST's resolve. The temple commissioned an artist named Chris Andres to design and build the monument and crowdfunded more than $12,000 to pay for it. The monument, which was completed in early summer of 2017, is a black steel rectangle measuring two feet by two feet by three feet, with embossed inverted golden pentagrams on each side and an upside-down soldier's helmet, also made from black steel, on the top. According to Andres, the helmet was designed to be used as a kind of bowl, for families and others to place messages to fallen veterans.

Once the monument was complete, the only thing left to do was for TST and the town to figure out when it would be installed. As the citizens of Belle Plaine began to realize that Satan was in fact coming to town, though, concern began to mount. A group of Catholics planned a rosary rally against the monument to be held at the park in mid-July. According to Robert Ritchie, director of America Needs Fatima, the national Catholic group that helped plan the rally: "Every time the devil is accepted, mankind is the loser, because he's only capable of doing evil. The more accepted he is, the more evil he will bring to us. And that's why it's important to pray against it." Members of Minnesota's Left Hand Path Community vowed to be present at the park on the same day to express their support for the contested monument.

Despite the controversy, TST continued to plan for the monument's installation. Over the course of researching this book, I've gotten to know a few members of the group, in particular its cofounder and spokesperson,

Lucien Greaves (whose real name is Doug Mesner). I contacted Mesner to find out if there were any concrete plans for moving the monument to Minnesota, so I could arrange to be there for the event, and he asked me if I'd be interested in helping to drive it there when it was ready. Really? Whoa! How exciting! I'd be embedded with TST like a journalist in an army unit during the Iraq War as one of the great moments in the nation's religious history played out.

Yes, I said. Definitely yes!

* * *

"Separation of church and state." It's one of the venerable phrases of our democratic experiment, right up there with "freedom of speech," "checks and balances," and "alternative facts."* Fleeing a despotic kingdom that had an official church, the framers of the Constitution were terrified of power overly concentrated in any one institution, and so they sought to separate religion and government in much the same way that they split power between the federal government and the states, or among the legislative, executive, and judicial branches. In his 1785 *Memorial and Remonstrance Against Religious Assessments*, the most important document from the founding era on the virtues of separating church and state, James Madison wrote about the perils of government support of religion, claiming that taxing the public to support Christian teaching would threaten the conscience of nonbelievers, encourage political tyranny, and undermine the vigor of religion itself. And Thomas Jefferson, in his 1802 letter to the Danbury Baptists, coined the famous phrase, when he observed that the Constitution had built "a wall of separation between Church and State." As a society, we have been debating just how high that wall should be ever since.

Despite its rhetorical appeal, the phrase "separation of church and state" does not appear anywhere in the Constitution itself. Nor does the Constitution say much at all about the specifics of that separation. What the Constitution does say about religion is almost entirely contained in

---

* "Alternative facts" is not actually one of the venerable phrases of our democratic experiment.

the first sentence of the First Amendment, which reads: "Congress shall make no law respecting an establishment of religion or prohibiting the free exercise thereof." The first part of that sentence is referred to as the "Establishment Clause," while the second is commonly called the "Free Exercise Clause." Both parts are critical to the concept of separating church and state, but when it comes to limiting government *support* of religion, rather than limiting government *regulation* of religion, it is the Establishment Clause that plays the most important role. But figuring out exactly what the clause means and how it should be applied to the countless ways that government and religion can potentially interact in our complex and diverse modern society is no easy task. In our constitutional democracy, the authority to interpret and apply the Constitution falls primarily to the courts, and ultimately to the Supreme Court of the United States. Operationally, then, the specific contours of the "separation of church and state" in this country have been set by the Supreme Court, which has interpreted and applied the Establishment Clause in a string of cases beginning in 1947 and continuing to the present day.

There was a time, primarily in the 1970s and 1980s, when the Supreme Court took the Establishment Clause a lot more seriously than it does today. It placed stringent limits on government funding of religion, for example, and largely kept religion out of the public schools. Over the past couple of decades, however, the Supreme Court has etched a new path of church-state relations and the First Amendment. In a series of cases, the Court has either expanded religion's right to access public money, property, and institutions, or it has confirmed what many hoped was religion's right to access these things.

For example, in the 2001 case of *Good News Club v. Milford Central School*, the Court held that if a public school opens up its classrooms to after-school groups, it cannot exclude religious groups from using them, even if the groups are actively proselytizing young children. In 2002, in the case of *Zelman v. Simmons-Harris*, the Court upheld a school voucher program that funneled millions of dollars to religious schools. The 2005 case of *Van Orden v. Perry* upheld the placement of a huge stone Ten Commandments monument right in front of the Texas State Capitol, and a 2014 case called *Town of Greece v. Galloway* held that town boards are free to begin their meetings with explicitly sectarian prayers. The nation's Christian majority has pounced on these and other decisions, putting up Christian displays on public property all over the country, giving prayers before town board meetings in every state, proselytizing young kids with after-school clubs in elementary schools across America, and using tons of government money to fund their organizations. I'm not sure it's accurate to say that the United States was ever really "separationist," but if it was, then the nation we live in now—with a few exceptions here and there—is pretty much a post-separationist one.

Alongside these legal developments, though, the nation has been experiencing another important change, this one demographic rather than legal. In recent years, the United States has become less and less Christian. Quantitative evidence of such a shift is always subject to legitimate quibbling, but at least one scholar has estimated that 98 percent of colonists in the revolutionary period were Christians, and that number, according to regular Gallup polls, remained above 90 percent as late as the early 1970s. As recently as 2007, the Pew Research Center, which is probably the preeminent authority on the demographics of religion in the United States, reported that 78.4 percent of American citizens described themselves as believing in some sort of Christianity. In Pew's 2014 comprehensive survey, however, that figure had declined to 70.6 percent. The nation is now more diverse than ever, with the share of Americans identifying with non-Christian faiths having risen to 5.9 percent at the time of that survey. Of particular interest is the number of people who describe themselves as not believing in God or a higher power at all. These "nones," according to Pew, made up nearly 22.8 percent of the population in 2014; a more recent study, from the Public Religion Research Institute, puts the number at 25 percent. In short, with nearly three out of every ten Americans now describing themselves as non-Christian, we are living in an increasingly non-Christian nation.

These two developments raise the inevitable question of what non-Christians are to do in this post-separationist America. As a longtime Atheist who has studied religion and feels an affinity for many minority religious traditions, particularly Taoism, Buddhism, and others that originated far away from the United States,[†] I've been thinking about this question for a while now. Three major possibilities come to mind. First, non-Christians could continue to fight in the courts to limit or even reverse some of the Supreme Court's anti-separationist precedents. Second, they could do basically nothing and go about their business, conceding that the fight for separationism is mostly lost and allowing the Christian majority to enjoy the spoils. Or finally, non-Christians could devote their energies to taking advantage of the Court's precedents and demanding their rightful place in American public life alongside the Christian majority. After all, although the Court's anti-separationist decisions all involve Christian attempts to access government money, property, and institutions, the Court has always maintained that the government must treat all religious views equally. If Christians can erect their monuments on public property and give invocations before town boards and run after-school proselytizing clubs and apply for government funding, then so too can non-Christians. Maybe that's what Atheists and members of minority religious groups ought to be doing.

Although many non-Christians continue to fight for separationism in the courts and others are content to go about their own business (there are costs to being supported by the government, after all), an increasing number of Atheists and minority religious believers have, in recent years, begun to pursue the third option and are starting to demand their rightful place in public life. Atheists have given invocations before town boards. A small religious group in Utah that believes in mummification asked a local park to put up their "Seven Aphorisms" monument next to the Ten Commandments. Pagans demanded that the Veterans Administration allow the Wiccan pentacle on gravestones at national cemeteries. Islamic schools

---

† Just a little biographical note, in case you're interested. I grew up Jewish, attending Hebrew School against my will until I was thirteen. It was early in high school that I first started identifying as an Atheist. I remember announcing this fact to my freshman English class, but then on the same day I broke my collarbone in gym class, so for a while there I kept my Atheism on the down-low. I was an East Asian studies major in college and wrote my senior thesis on a quirky Taoist sage named Chuang Tzu. Later I got a master's degree in religious studies at the University of Chicago Divinity School. I would have pursued a doctorate in Chinese religions, but when I realized that my Chinese language skills were not really good enough to read a simple children's story, much less decipher sophisticated ancient religious texts, I left grad school and took the LSAT.

from Cleveland to North Carolina have participated in voucher programs and received hundreds of thousands of dollars from the government. Scientologists and Hare Krishnas have accepted funds from federal agencies to provide services to believers and nonbelievers alike. And Satanists have done everything from giving prayers before government bodies to asking towns for permission to install their monuments to creating after-school clubs to counter the efforts of aggressive Christian organizations.

The primary purpose of this book is to explain and explore this fascinating and important new phenomenon. In a series of chapters about religious monuments, sectarian displays, legislative prayers, government funding, and extracurricular activities in the public schools, I will detail both how the Supreme Court has largely torn down the wall of separation between church and state and how Atheists and other non-Christians have taken advantage of this post-separationist legal regime to participate in public life alongside the Christian majority.‡ I will also report on how the government and the Christian majority have responded to such demands by non-Christians. At times the response has been tolerant and even, occasionally, welcoming. But more often than not, the response has been distressingly hostile, ignorant, and hateful. Non-Christian displays have been torn down, invocations interrupted, requests for money met with disgust and hostility. Occasionally, the government has decided to exclude religion entirely from some public space rather than allow Christianity to share the stage with other religious and nonreligious views.

Most of my accounts and descriptions of events are drawn from public reporting, but I have also attempted, wherever possible, to travel and talk with key individuals and groups to learn as much as I could about their

---

‡   A quick but important definitional point: Obviously, religious groups can "participate in public life" in all sorts of ways, from taking part in debates about public policy to giving away literature to holding rituals and other activities in public areas like parks. In this book, however, I will use the phrases "participation in public life," "participating in the public square," "demanding a place in public life," and similar formulations specifically to refer to taking advantage of the Supreme Court's anti-separationist decisions on religious monuments and displays, legislative prayers, government funding of religion, and religion in the public schools to gain access to government money, property, and institutions.

motivations. I watched an Atheist who had previously sued her town without success to stop it from allowing Christian prayers before its board meetings give a secular invocation in upstate New York, met with D.C.-area Wiccans who every Memorial Day hold small ceremonies at each of the eight graves marked with a Wiccan pentacle in the National Cemetery, and spent a weekend at a conference in Ohio learning about the movement to spread secular student groups on campuses around the country. I hung out with the quirky religious group called the Summum in its Utah pyramid filled with mummies and sat on the lap of a $100,000 bronze statue of a goat-headed figure named Baphomet that the Satanic Temple hopes someday to place on government property. In the course of my conversations and travels, I learned why Selena Fox and members of the Circle Sanctuary, her Wisconsin Wiccan community, felt so strongly about getting the Department of Veterans Affairs to allow those pentacles on National Cemetery graves. I traveled to Raleigh, North Carolina, to meet with Mussarut Jabeen, the principal of an Islamic elementary and middle school, about how school vouchers have helped her school thrive. And I spoke at length with Doug Mesner from the Satanic Temple about why his group believes it is crucial to demand equal access to government property and institutions. My goal in connecting with these people was always to learn why they fought to have their voices heard, how the fight affected them, and whether they think the fight was worth fighting. Their stories are surprising, fascinating, and inspiring.

Although the book is largely descriptive, it also advances an argument that I believe is extremely important, namely, that given the Supreme Court's church-state jurisprudence, the trend I describe is one that those of us who value a diverse and pluralistic society should welcome, celebrate, and encourage. I will argue that non-Christians who want to participate in public life are right to push for access to the public square and should continue to demand their equal place there. In the six descriptive chapters of the book and a substantive concluding chapter, I will contend, for example, that non-Christians should insist on joining Christians in giving invocations before town hall meetings and the national legislature. They should fight to erect their monuments on public property next to the crosses and the Ten Commandments. They should run schools and compete for public voucher funding. They should take whatever opportunities they can to spread their messages in the public schools whenever Christians are doing the same. Only by insisting on exercising these rights can Muslims, Hindus, Buddhists, Atheists, and everybody else ensure that the Court's new religion jurisprudence does not result in a public space occupied exclusively by Christian messages and symbols.

At stake is nothing less than the future of our national public life. With more and more Americans claiming allegiance to minority religions and an increasing number of people embracing nonbelief as an affirmative alternative to religion, the United States currently stands at a critical juncture. The decisions that religious groups and public officials make now will shape the nature of the public square for years to come. Will public life continue to be dominated by Christian voices? Will the Christian majority decide that no voices are better than all voices, resulting in a public square empty of all religion? Or will minority religious believers and nonbelievers insist on their right to participate in public life alongside the Christian majority and find a majority willing to invite them in, thus creating a public square filled with voices of every type and stripe?

There are a number of reasons that a public square filled with the voices of all sorts of religious believers, as well as those of nonbelievers who have strong feelings about the questions traditionally addressed by religion, would be preferable to one dominated exclusively by Christian voices. For one thing, it would be more consistent with American ideals of inclusivity and freedom of speech represented by the First Amendment. As a nation, we have long been devoted to the idea that all citizens have the right to express their opinions, exchange ideas, and participate in public life. A public square filled with religious voices of all sorts better fits with this idea than the alternative does.

Second, the presence of a multitude of views on religious questions in the public square will help educate all Americans about the diversity of religious belief and practice that exists within the nation and around the world. If minority religious believers express their beliefs exclusively in private, how will others understand them? A person may not know anything about Druidism, for example, but if he or she sees a Druid give a prayer in public, or studies a lesson in school about Druidism, or even sees a monument put up by a Druid on public property, that person will know that Druidism exists in the community and will learn at least a little bit about what it means to be a Druid. The same goes for Hinduism or Islam. And I believe that the more we as a society understand minority religions, the more likely we are to learn to treat one another with mutual understanding and respect instead of with stereotypes, ignorance, and hatred. This is true not only here in the United States but also around the globe. Participating thoughtfully and meaningfully in international affairs requires an understanding of other people's religions (how can we understand anything about the Middle East, for example, without understanding something about Islam?). It may be hard to see how erecting a Satanic monument in a public park might lead, however slightly, to a more peaceful world, but that's exactly what I plan to suggest in this book.

* * *

Before diving into the details, I want to pause for a moment to address two big-picture issues—one a question, the other an objection—that have come up repeatedly as I've talked to people about this project over the past couple of years.

First, the question: When I say that "non-Christians" should demand access to public life, what do I mean by that term? Who is it that I'm talking about? The answer is this: Basically, I'm talking about any group of people who hold sincere beliefs about the fundamental nature of the world that happen to differ from those of the Christian majority. More specifically, though, I would like to highlight a few separate points.

Initially, I want to make clear that of course not all Christians are the same. There are many, many (many!) different varieties of Christianity. Catholics are not the same as Lutherans, who are not the same as Baptists, and so on. Moreover, the same denomination often encompasses different schools of thought and views about all sorts of different issues. Some Catholics believe women should be ordained as priests; others don't. Some Protestants believe the world was created in seven days and the earth is flat; most don't. Some Episcopalians believe that gay marriage is fine; others don't. Finally, Christians vary in how seriously they take their faith, from evangelicals who actively proselytize to those who go to church only on

Easter. Although I won't focus on them in this book, if there are groups of Christians in the United States who hold minority views that they believe are underrepresented in the public square, by all means those groups should take advantage of the Supreme Court's decisions on church and state as much as anybody else.

Second, Atheists and other "nones" are most definitely included. Atheism (and to be accurate, I should note that Atheism is hardly monolithic either—some people who do not believe in the existence of any divine being refer to themselves as "Freethinkers" or "Secularists" or "Humanists" rather than "Atheists," and each category has its own nuances) provides answers to the same questions that Christianity attempts to answer, even if it answers those questions in a way that is radically different from the way that Christianity or most other religions answer them. Since this book is about people and communities that possess strong and sincere beliefs that differ from those of the Christian majority and would like to bring those beliefs into the public square, it would make no sense to arbitrarily exclude Atheists and other nonbelievers from the discussion. A public square that is truly inclusive on issues that are at the heart of Christianity must include views that deny or reject the core assumptions of religion as well as views that are religious but non-Christian. For instance, if the public square is to be inclusive on the question of who or what is the creative force behind the universe, it has to include as one alternative among many the notion that there is no such force whatsoever as well as the belief that there is a single god with a son named Jesus. Likewise, when it comes to ethics, why would we include alternatives to Christian biblical ethics from other religious traditions but not the Humanist notion that ethical obligations stem from the nature of being human itself?

Third and finally, although I will of course use the word "religion" (and other versions of the term) nearly constantly, nothing in the book's argument turns on any kind of specific definition of what counts as "religion," and therefore I will not advance and defend any particular definition of the term as authoritative. The point of the book, after all, is that the public square should include alternatives to Christian views, so it does not matter if those alternatives are in any technical sense "religious" or not.

This is a big load off my mind, I should admit, because trying to formulate a satisfying definition of "religion" is nearly impossible. For one thing, what kind of definition would we want? Legal? Anthropological? Sociological? Theological? Moreover, what most people think of as being "religious" simply defies simple definition. Seriously, try to define the term and see if you can come up with an acceptable formulation, one that captures all the belief systems you think are religious and excludes all those that aren't. Should we define a "religion" as a belief system that has a certain *content*, like a belief in a Supreme Being? If so, then what about traditions, like Taoism, that lack such a being? Do we instead define "religion" as any belief system that fulfills a certain *function* in a person's life, such as any belief that is a person's "ultimate concern"? If so, then on what basis would we exclude from the definition something like the love of college football, which for some people might meet the same needs that Christianity does for a devout believer?

The Supreme Court, perhaps recognizing the difficulty of defining religion, has never done so, even though the word appears right there in the First Amendment. Lower courts, which sometimes have no choice but to come up with something, generally just say that a "religion" is any comprehensive belief system that addresses fundamental questions and that looks pretty much like what we think "religion" looks like—one with rituals, holidays, a system of ethics, sacred texts, officiants, and other characteristics of mainstream religions. In other words, they take a "we know it when we see it" approach. This type of analogical definition is hardly satisfying, of course, but in my view it is probably the best of the alternatives, and if I were pressed, it is the kind of approach to defining "religion" that I would adopt.

Okay, so that's the question. As for the objection, it comes from hardcore separationists, generally people on the far left of the political spectrum who are deeply suspicious of religion, particularly of conservative strands of Christianity. These objectors suggest that there's no way to have a truly pluralistic public square filled with lots of different religious voices because Christian voices will always dominate and squelch those with competing views. According to this position, the only acceptable solution is a public square that is almost entirely secular, one in which people do not rely on their religious views when making arguments about public policy, much less erect religious monuments on public property or pray before town board meetings.

The objection is exemplified by the reaction I got from a colleague who attended a faculty workshop where I presented an early version of the book. This colleague, who is ordinarily extremely thoughtful, fair, and scholarly, and with whom I am friendly, listened to my presentation and then when it was her turn to comment, declared, "I'm sorry, but I think this is insane." Whoa! I mean, I know my work is deeply, deeply flawed, but is it really *insane*? When the laughter died down, my colleague explained that having grown up in a conservative part of the United States, she could not imagine how my proposed inclusive public square could possibly work. All non-Christian voices, she asserted, would be handily drowned out by those in the majority.

Fair enough. It is certainly possible that she, and those who agree with her, are correct. We won't know if a healthy pluralistic public square is possible until we actually try to create one. Perhaps Christian voices will invariably dominate to such a degree that nobody else will ever be truly heard. Maybe instead of understanding and tolerance, a more diverse public square will simply result in more of the same—misunderstanding, indifference, even hostility. Perhaps things will become more chaotic in the short term, but more peaceful in the long term. Or vice versa. Although I will try to make the case throughout this book that there are good reasons to be optimistic, ultimately whether a healthy, pluralistic public square is possible is an empirical question that I simply cannot answer definitively in these pages.

But I will repeat here what I said to my colleague: The question of whether a public square filled with a cacophony of religious and non-religious voices is preferable to a fully secular public square is simply *irrelevant*, because the Supreme Court has already rejected the possibility of a secular public square. Whatever the merits may be of a society in which religion and government are kept largely separate, such a society does not exist today in the United States and will likely not emerge at any time in the near future. Thanks to the Court, our society is one in which the government can support religion in all sorts of ways, including giving it boatloads of money and access to public property and institutions.

Christians are already taking advantage of these decisions and have been for some time. *Thus, the only question that really matters is whether a public square filled with a wide variety of religious and non-religious voices is better than one filled solely with Christian voices.* And that, I believe, for anyone who cares at all about pluralism, is a question that answers itself.

Indeed, active participation by Atheists and other minorities in public life may ironically turn out to be the best hope for creating a secular public square in the United States. As we'll see throughout the book, many predominantly Christian communities, when faced with demands by minorities to give invocations before local boards or to distribute religious materials in the public schools or to erect their own displays and monuments, have chosen to bar religious participation in public life completely rather than allowing minorities to participate alongside Christians. My argument in favor of minority participation in public life does not rely on this result—as I'll explain more thoroughly in the book's conclusion, I think that either an entirely secular or a religiously cacophonous public square is preferable to an exclusively Christian one—but I think its possibility should go some way toward satisfying those readers who can't imagine any religiously clothed public square where Christian voices don't drown out the voices of minorities.

When I first started working on this book back in 2015, the situation was not nearly as clear-cut as it is now. During that year, and throughout most of 2016, it looked possible, if not likely, that Hillary Clinton was going to win the presidency. Had that happened, Clinton would probably have been able to fill several Supreme Court vacancies with justices sympathetic to the notion of separating church and state. Had such a Supreme Court actually been put in place, it might have made more sense for non-Christians to focus their efforts on getting the law regarding government support of religion changed through litigation rather than on getting their voices heard in the public square. The question of whether a secular public square would be better than one filled with a variety of religious voices would have been an important one to address.

But of course, Hillary Clinton did not win the 2016 election. Donald Trump swept the Rust Belt and took the presidency in January 2017, essentially ending any chance in the near term for reversing the Court's jurisprudence concerning the separation of church and state. Trump filled the seat left vacant by Justice Antonin Scalia's death (and Mitch McConnell's reprehensible, indefensible refusal to let Merrick Garland's appointment come to a vote in the Senate) with Neil Gorsuch, who demonstrated his right-wing leanings within months of taking the seat. If any doubt remained about which way the Court would turn, Senator Susan Collins quashed it when she voted to confirm the far-right Brett Kavanaugh for the seat vacated by Justice Anthony Kennedy, despite the fact that credible claims of sexual assault had been leveled against the nominee. The chances that the Court will now reverse course on the Establishment Clause are basically zilch. With a constitutionally required secular public square out of the question, the only real alternative for non-Christians is to demand their rightful place alongside Christians in public life.

At the same time, though, Trump's election and what it represents make the project that is at the center of this book more important than ever. Of course, it has never been easy to be a minority in the United States, but it feels harder now more than at any time in recent memory. Minorities of all kinds—whether with respect to race, gender, nationality, religion, or sexual orientation—have fallen under attack in Trump's America. The president's hateful actions and rhetoric have reverberated far outside Washington; hate crimes and hateful speech aimed at minorities have skyrocketed, as some Trump supporters feel vindicated by their president and freed to speak their minds. In such an atmosphere, it is crucial for minorities of all types, including religious minorities, to speak up against policies that would shut them out and to insist that they receive equal respect as citizens. The need for non-Christians to demand their rightful place in public life has never been more urgent.

* * *

So, did I get to help drive the Satanic monument to Minnesota? Did the Satanists end up erecting the monument in Veterans Memorial Park? Was the monument met with widespread rioting? Read on, and I promise you will soon find out.

1

MUMMIES, MONUMENTS, AND MONOTHEISM

Religious Displays as Government Speech

IN THE LATE 1970S, an administrative manager for a Salt Lake City supply company, Corky Ra, founded a small religious group called the Summum after he was visited by advanced beings from another planet who conveyed to him lessons that are now known as the tradition's "Seven Aphorisms." Among these aphorisms are "The Principle of Psychokinesis," which holds that "the universe is a mental creation," and "The Principle of Vibration," which says that "nothing rests, everything moves, everything vibrates." The members of the Summum believe that the first set of stone tablets received by Moses on the top of Mount Sinai in fact contained the Seven Aphorisms, but that when Moses saw the immaturity of his people, he smashed those tablets, returned to the summit of Sinai, got the Ten Commandments, and gave those to the people instead.

Pleasant Grove, Utah, is a small town nestled at the foot of Mount Timpanogos and some other beautiful peaks that are snow-tipped even in the early summertime. Across from the building that houses the town's government lies a little historical site called Pioneer Park, and within that park sits a monument to the Ten Commandments. In the late 1990s, the Summum decided that if it was okay for the park to have a Ten Commandments monument, then it should also have a Seven Aphorisms monument, since, after all, the Seven Aphorisms are really the completion of the message received by Moses on the top of Mount Sinai. The town did not agree. The Summum sued, and the case went all the way to the United States Supreme Court, which held in favor of the town and against the quirky religious group.

The Summum is a fascinating organization, with a number of eclectic beliefs and practices. Its belief that God gave Corky Ra and not Moses the tablet containing the most important of his teachings is only the beginning. Like many religious traditions, the Summum places great emphasis on the practice of meditation, and, although its extremely well-done website concedes that "there are no incorrect forms of meditation," it also suggests that the particular type of meditation practiced by the Summum is superior. Specifically, the website suggests that the "Summum Transcending Meditations," if done correctly, with the proper training and materials, will result in "pure, alert, clear, total, undisturbed, and OPEN consciousness," in which "your attention vibrates and harmonizes with this consciousness." In addition, the group brews its own alcoholic "nectars" on-site in its pyramid and uses these nectars (also known as "publications") as part of its meditation practice. Each nectar (there are nine so far, including one for "devotion," one for "cause and effect," and—my favorite—one for "nothing") "carries its own message" "across the blood-brain barrier," where it is "transmitted to the brain on a molecular level" and eventually, with "continued use . . . brings about a change in your perception."

Probably the most interesting aspect of the Summum, however, is a belief in mummification. This is also the group's most well-known practice, as it has been featured on a number of national news programs, including *Good Morning America*. The basis for the belief has to do with making the transition between life and death go more smoothly. According to an essay on the Summum website titled, "Mummification . . . A Philosophical Examination":

> Whereupon you die and leave your body, it is not so much an end as it is a continuous flow leading to a new beginning or rebirth. Although you have left your body, you remain capable of feelings and are very much aware of the incidents taking place, for your attention remains intact. . . . The change, however, is normally a frightening and puzzling

experience. Your sense of time and space has changed. Your essence (which is really you) finds itself in a very unfamiliar situation. . . . Most people are buried or cremated and this places their essence in less than favorable circumstances leaving it to fend for itself. In mummification, the preserved body serves as a reference point for your essence, a "home base" if you will that allows communication of instructions to help guide you to your new destination. This can alleviate much of the fear, anxiety, and confusion that you would normally experience.

The group offers its mummification services to the general public. For a fee of $67,000 (more for larger adults), you can arrange for your own mummification, a process performed by "mummification experts" who bathe your dead body and remove internal organs to a "baptismal font filled with a special preservation solution made up of certain fluids, some of which are chemicals used in genetic engineering" for a significant period of time, after which your organs are put back into your body and you are wrapped in several layers of cotton and perhaps even some silk. The experts, including people called thanatogeneticists, will then apply a polymer membrane to the wrappings, followed by a layer of fiberglass resin, before taking your body inside the pyramid, where it will be given the rites of Transference. After this, your body will be placed inside a capsule called a mummiform and stored in a mausoleum or sanctuary for eternity. You can choose or design the mummiform you would like to be placed in (you have to make this choice while you're alive, of course), but be careful when doing so because this decision can add quite a bit to the final bill. According to the Summum website, artistic mummiforms "vary widely in cost, from tens of thousands of dollars to well over a hundred thousand dollars depending on how elaborate they are."

It is unclear to me how many people have in fact taken advantage of these services—how many besides Corky Ra, that is, who is mummified and stored in an elaborate (and presumably quite expensive) artistic mummiform inside the Summum pyramid itself. According to an admittedly old segment of *CBS Evening News* with a link on the group's website, fourteen hundred people have already paid for their future mummification. That same video, however, indicates that pet mummification pays the bills, and indeed the website provides all sorts of specifications for having one's pet mummified. A standard bronze mummiform for a normal-size cat (less than fifteen pounds) will set you back only four thousand bucks.*

I think you will probably understand from my description of the Summum why I wanted to visit the group. In the late spring of 2016, I bought a plane ticket and headed out to Salt Lake City.

* * *

"Congress shall make no law respecting an establishment of religion." Nothing about the meaning of this constitutional provision is obvious. What is an "establishment of religion"? What counts as "religion"? What in the world does the word "respecting" mean? Some of the framers of the Constitution certainly had opinions about what these words meant, but their viewpoints were hardly universally shared, and in any event, the nation is so different now—and the issues so much more complex than they were in the eighteenth century—that those same positions can hardly be considered authoritative today.† As a result, it has been the United States Supreme Court that has defined the meaning of the Establishment Clause ever since the 1940s.

Perhaps unsurprisingly, given the complexity of the issues, the Court itself has not always been clear or consistent in how it has interpreted and applied the Establishment Clause to the vast variety of cases that have come before it. The Court has developed a number of legal "tests" to evaluate any alleged violation of the clause, most notably the *Lemon*

---

*   The mummification materials on the Summum website are so fascinating that I'm tempted to devote several chapters to them alone. Since this book isn't about mummification, though, I'm going to resist that temptation. I can't, however, stop myself from at least mentioning the part of the website aimed at kids and featuring "Mummy Bear," who is described as a "small, fluffy bear" born in Atlantis in the year 26,486 B.C. "Mummy Bear" takes part in many adventures, tells stories, reads poems, sings songs, and tells mummy-related jokes, like this one: "Why was the mummy so tense?" "Because he was all wound up."

†   There are those, of course, who would disagree with this statement, but I'm not going to defend the point here. For a comprehensive critique of all forms of "originalism," I recommend taking a look at James Fleming's *Fidelity to Our Imperfect Constitution*, published by Oxford University Press in 2015.

test, which says that for a government action to be constitutional, it must have a predominantly secular purpose and must not have the primary effect of promoting or advancing religion. Although the Court has formally applied this test to all sorts of cases under the Establishment Clause, it is in fact so vague as to be practically useless by itself. To understand what the Court is really doing in any particular type of church/state dispute, whether you're interested in money or prayer or the school curriculum or what have you, the best thing to do is to look at the cases in that specific area and see what the Court actually has done.

When it comes to evaluating the constitutionality of religious symbols, displays, and monuments, the real legal standard has been the "endorsement test," which asks whether the government has endorsed a particular religion or even endorsed religion over non-religion. The test was developed by Justice O'Connor in the 1980s, and it forbids the government from either acting with the purpose of endorsing religion or conveying a message of endorsement, even without any intention to endorse religion. On this latter point, Justice O'Connor explained, "What is crucial is that a government practice not have the effect of communicating a message of government endorsement or disapproval of religion. It is only practices having that effect, whether intentionally or unintentionally, that make religion relevant, in reality or public perception, to status in the political community." Justice O'Connor's fear was that when the government endorses religion, it sends "a message to non-adherents that they are outsiders, not full members of the political community, and an accompanying message to adherents that they are insiders, favored members of the political community." The test complicates matters by requiring courts to consider the symbol or display from the perspective of a "reasonable person," one who is familiar with the full context of the challenged symbol, including its meaning, its history, and the specific circumstances that resulted in its display by the government.

At a general level, the test is a good one, at least in my opinion, but if you look at it more closely and think about how courts have to apply it in practice, its difficulties quickly become apparent. Who is this "reasonable person"? How can a judge or justice imagine what such a person would think or feel when viewing any specific display? Since judges in the United

States come predominantly from the Judeo-Christian traditions, can they really be trusted to dispassionately discern how a Judeo-Christian display might affect someone who holds non-Judeo-Christian beliefs—a Buddhist or Scientologist, for example, or an Atheist?

The two cases in which Justice O'Connor first articulated the endorsement test illustrate some of the test's weaknesses. The first case—*Lynch v. Donnelly*, from 1984—involved a challenge to a crèche placed on public property in Pawtucket, Rhode Island. The Court held 5–4 in favor of the government. The plurality opinion was written by Justice Burger, whose "reasoning" was characteristically glib and dopey. Justice O'Connor wrote a concurrence in which she articulated and applied her test, finding that the display was constitutional. Key to her reasoning was the physical setting of the crèche, which was surrounded by a bunch of silly, non-religious items like candy-striped poles, reindeer, a clown, and an elephant. According to Justice O'Connor, the town had merely intended to celebrate public holidays of cultural significance (predominant secular purpose), and the "overall holiday setting" of the crèche "negate[d] any message of endorsement" of the display's religious content (no primary effect of advancing religion).

Even more weird was the 1989 follow-up, *County of Allegheny v. ACLU*. That case involved two separate displays—a crèche positioned all by itself, completely sans reindeer and clowns, on the steps of a courthouse, and a forty-foot Christmas tree next to an eighteen-foot menorah in front of a sign proclaiming "Salute to Liberty." For the first time, five members of the Court applied Justice O'Connor's endorsement test. For these justices, the crèche was easy. Unaccompanied by candy canes, elephants, or clowns, the clearly religious symbol sent an unconstitutional message of endorsement.

The other display, however, inspired more disagreement among the five justices who applied the endorsement test. Justices Brennan, Stevens, and Marshall thought that the display endorsed religion over non-religion, Judeo-Christian religions over other religions, and Christianity over Judaism (because the tree was so much taller than the menorah). On the other hand, Justice Blackmun took the position that since the Christmas tree (a secular symbol) in this display was so much bigger than the menorah, the Christmas tree transformed the menorah from a religious symbol to a secular one, resulting in a display that simply celebrated both Christmas and Hanukkah in a secular fashion. On the *other* hand, Justice O'Connor, although she explicitly disagreed with Justice Blackmun that the menorah could be understood as anything other than a religious symbol, nonetheless still thought that the display was okay because the sign made it clear that the whole scene was merely sending a message of pluralism and liberty. The combination of the votes of Justice O'Connor and Justice Blackmun with those of the four justices who didn't think that endorsement should be the test at all (they would have upheld any display that did not in fact *coerce* nonbelievers into changing their beliefs) resulted in a 6–3 decision upholding the display.

The endorsement test is one of the Court's more maligned pieces of constitutional jurisprudence. Not only does it arguably have all the problems I identified earlier—it is vague, difficult to apply in a principled fashion, and biased in favor of majority religions—but it also, as the *Lynch* and *Allegheny* decisions demonstrate, kind of makes the Court look ridiculous and the justices like a bunch of highfalutin goofballs. One influential lower-court judge once famously said that the test "resembles interior decorating more than constitutional law." Do we really want our justices arguing about whether a giant Christmas tree makes a smaller menorah secular, or rather, as Justice Brennan argued, the menorah, by being so clearly a religious symbol, makes the Christmas tree religious as well?

Personally, I'd prefer a nice clear rule prohibiting all government-sponsored religious displays and symbols on public property. That is highly unlikely ever to happen, though, and so for now, the endorsement test is probably the next best thing. It at least serves to keep some of the more egregious sectarian symbols from receiving the approval and imprimatur of the government, which, after all, is supposed to be acting on behalf of all of us, not just those who happen to believe that Jesus is the son of God. But be warned: As this book is going to press, the Supreme Court has agreed to hear a case involving a forty-foot World War I monument in the shape of a cross that could change or even eliminate the endorsement test.

* * *

This, then, brings us to the Ten Commandments. Of course, since there are multiple versions of the Ten Commandments—a Jewish one, a Catholic one, and so on, you might think that the public display of any specific version would count as an unconstitutional endorsement of that version, but the justices have not generally looked at the question in quite so sophisticated a fashion. Instead they have asked whether any particular display of the Ten Commandments promotes Judeo-Christian religion generally over other religions or no religion. Three times the Court has taken up challenges involving the Ten Commandments, and I'm kind of happy to report that the challengers have a 2–1 record. The first case—*Stone v. Graham*, from 1980, involving a Kentucky state law requiring that a copy of the Ten Commandments be posted in every public school classroom—predated the creation of the endorsement test and was struck down because the Court thought the state law was motivated solely to promote religion and therefore lacked a predominant secular purpose under the *Lemon* test. The other two cases, however, each decided on the same day in 2005, are more relevant to the topic at hand.

The first of these was *McCreary County v. ACLU of Kentucky*. That case involved a couple of counties in Kentucky that posted copies of the Ten Commandments in public areas of their courthouses. The facts of the case were convoluted. At first, clearly motivated by an intent to promote religion, the counties put up large copies of the Ten Commandments in gold frames displayed all by themselves on the courthouse walls. After the ACLU sued, however, the counties changed the arrangement so that the Ten Commandments were surrounded by the religious portions of eight other historical documents, such as the part of the Declaration of Independence that talks about the Creator and President Lincoln's 1863 Proclamation of a Day of Prayer and Humiliation. When the counties removed these displays in response to a court order, they replaced them once again, this time positioning the Ten Commandments alongside the full versions of eight other historical documents, including the Mayflower Compact and a picture of Lady Justice. The counties titled these collections "The Foundations of American Law and Government Display" and included the Ten Command-ments because they "provide the moral background of the Declaration of Independence and the foundation of our legal tradition."

The Court struck down this final display by a 5–4 margin. Key to Justice Souter's analysis in the majority opinion was the notion that a reasonable observer would remember the original reason that the counties had put the Ten Commandments up in the first place—to promote religion. The counties argued that the Court should look only at the final version of the display, which they suggested was purely secular. Justice Souter disagreed:

> [T]he world is not made brand new every morning, and the Counties are simply asking us to ignore perfectly probative evidence; they want an absentminded objective observer, not one presumed to be familiar with the history of the government's actions and competent to learn what history has to show. . . . The Counties' position just bucks common sense: reasonable observers have reasonable memories.

The dissent was written by Justice Scalia and joined by Chief Justice Rehnquist and Justices Thomas and Kennedy, although only Rehnquist and Thomas joined the part of Scalia's opinion that is one of the most obnoxious pieces of drivel ever put forward by members of the Court in a First Amendment case involving religion. In that part of the opinion, Scalia argued that since our nation has had a long history of acknowledging a single deity through official statements like "In God We Trust" on our money, it follows that the government is free to promote monotheistic religion over both non-religion and polytheism without violating the First Amendment.

"[I]t is entirely clear from our Nation's historical practices," the characteristically nasty Scalia wrote, "that the Establishment Clause permits this disregard of polytheists and believers in unconcerned deities, just as it permits the disregard of devout atheists." Furthermore, since 97.7 percent of religious believers in the United States are monotheists and believe that the Ten Commandments "are divine prescriptions for a virtuous life," displaying those Commandments cannot, according to Scalia, "be reasonably understood as a government endorsement of a religious viewpoint." I imagine that Justice Stevens was probably softly weeping into his handkerchief when he responded to this twaddle by pointing out that Scalia was "marginalizing the belief systems of more than 7 million Americans by deeming them unworthy of the special protections he offers monotheists." As Justice O'Connor further (and rightly) explained: "It is true that many Americans find the Commandments in accord with their personal beliefs. But we do not count heads before enforcing the First Amendment."

The second Ten Commandments case involved a challenge to a huge (six feet by three feet) granite monument on the grounds of the Texas State Capitol. For forty years after it had been donated to the state by the Fraternal Order of Eagles, the monument stood between the capitol building and the Texas Supreme Court. At the time of the lawsuit, which was brought by a homeless lawyer who passed the monument nearly every day on his way from the tent where he slept to the Supreme Court, where he did his work, the capitol grounds were also home to sixteen other monuments meant to commemorate the "people, ideals, and events that compose Texan identity," including one to the heroes of the Alamo and another to the children of the state.

In the case of *Van Orden v. Perry*, the Court ruled in favor of the government. Four justices voted to uphold the monument for the reasons given in Chief Justice Rehnquist's plurality opinion. According to Rehnquist, the case was fairly easy—the monument was just one more chapter of "the unbroken history of official acknowledgement by all three branches of government of the role of religion in American life from at least 1789." The fact that the Ten Commandments are religious did not mean, for these four justices, that displaying them would be any more unconstitutional than displaying George Washington's Thanksgiving Proclamation or the image of Moses on the south frieze of the Supreme Court's own courtroom. "[T]he Ten Commandments have an undeniable historical meaning," Rehnquist wrote. "Simply having religious content or promoting a message consistent with a religious doctrine does not run afoul of the Establishment Clause."

Four other justices dissented for the reasons provided in the opinions of Justices Souter and Stevens. For these justices, the monument clearly endorsed religion over non-religion as well as monotheism over its alternatives and therefore violated the government's obligation to remain neutral on questions of religious faith. As Justice Souter put it, "A governmental display of an obviously religious text cannot be squared with neutrality, except in a setting that plausibly indicates that the statement is not placed in view with a predominant purpose on the part of government either to adopt the religious message or to urge its acceptance by others." With regard to the setting of this particular display, Justice Souter and the justices who agreed with him pointed to, among other things, the fact that the monument is a "permanent fixture at the seat of Texas government" (Justice Stevens), which is "the civic home of every one of the State's citizens" (Justice Souter). According to Souter, "[i]f neutrality in religion means something, any citizen should be able to visit that civic home without having to confront religious expressions clearly meant to convey an official religious position that may be at odds with his own religion, or with rejection of religion."

As I've described it so far, the lineup of the justices in *Van Orden* was exactly the same as in *McCreary*, which of course came out against the government rather than in its favor. The difference between the decision in *McCreary* and the decision in *Van Orden* was Justice Breyer, who voted to strike down the *McCreary* display but to uphold the *Van Orden* monument. When the Court decides a case like this—with four on one side and four on the other and a narrow concurrence making the difference, it is the concurrence that typically creates the controlling law. Unfortunately for everyone concerned, Justice Breyer's short opinion is largely inscrutable and completely unsatisfying. For Breyer, the excruciatingly indeterminate and unpredictable endorsement test was just not quite indeterminate and unpredictable enough. Instead, Breyer wrote that in hard cases such as this one, "no exact formula can dictate a resolution" and there can be "no test-related substitute for the exercise of legal judgment."

Exercising his "legal judgment," Justice Breyer looked to some of the different circumstances surrounding the monument and decided what he thought was important and what wasn't. In ruling for the government, Breyer emphasized the physical setting of the monument in a park surrounded by many other monuments and historical markers. For Breyer, this was a setting that "does not readily lend itself to meditation or any other religious activity" but "does provide a context of history and moral ideals," a point forcefully rebutted by Justice Souter, who argued that "17 monuments with no common appearance, history, or esthetic role scattered over 22 acres is not a museum, and anyone strolling around the lawn would surely take each memorial on its own terms without any dawning sense that some purpose held the miscellany together more coherently than fortuity and the edge of the grass." Most important for Breyer, though, was the fact that the monument had stood for forty years without apparently causing any controversy or attracting any legal challenge. "[T]hose forty years," Breyer wrote, "suggest more strongly than can any set of formulaic tests that few individuals, whatever their system of beliefs, are likely to have understood the monument as amounting, in any significantly detrimental way, to a government effort to favor a particular religious sect [or] primarily to promote religion over nonreligion." Justice Souter responded to this by pointing out that given how difficult, costly, and risky it is to bring a lawsuit like this one against the government, "I doubt that a slow walk to the courthouse, even one that took 40 years, is much evidentiary help in applying the Establishment Clause." Once again, Souter's point was dead-on, but unfortunately, it did not carry the day.

So, what then is the significance of the Court's decision in *Van Orden*? Are Ten Commandments monuments on public property constitutional under the Establishment Clause? As a general matter, all we can say is, "Who knows?" All we really know, given Justice Breyer's weird little opinion, is that a monument donated by a private organization, placed near seventeen other monuments so the area seems sort of like a museum, and standing for forty years without being challenged is probably constitutional. What, you might ask, if the monument were surrounded by only ten other monuments rather than seventeen? Who knows? What if the monument had been around for only thirty-nine years? Ten years? One day? It certainly appears that the newer the monument, the more likely Justice Breyer would be to hold it unconstitutional, but ultimately nobody knows for sure.

In the years since the Supreme Court decided *McCreary* and *Van Orden*, lower courts have struggled to figure out whether various Ten Commandments monuments and displays have violated the Constitution. The cases come out all over the place; some uphold Ten Commandments monuments, and others strike them down. For instance, a 2009 case from the Eighth Circuit Court of Appeals upheld a monument in a Plattsmouth, Nebraska, park even though it was not surrounded by other monuments, on the grounds that it was placed in a "relatively isolated corner" of the park and had been there for forty-plus years without anyone challenging it. On the other hand, the Tenth Circuit Court of Appeals struck down a similar monument that was erected in 2010 in the Municipal Complex of Bloomfield, New Mexico, on the grounds that it was not long-standing, even though it was surrounded by monuments depicting the Declaration of Independence, the Bill of Rights, and the Gettysburg Address. In 2008, the Ninth Circuit Court of Appeals upheld a monument in Everett, Washington, because, among other things, it was "surrounded by trees and shrubs."

* * *

The Summum's headquarters are located on Genesee Avenue in a nondescript neighborhood on the west side of Salt Lake City. I could give you the exact address, but you might as well just drive down the street and look for the lot with the giant pyramid on it. Don't worry, there's only one. I found it quite easily when I visited Salt Lake to see if I could find out why the Summum wanted to get its monument put up next to the Ten Commandments.

The group offers "classes" open to the public each Wednesday evening, so I headed over there one night to see what I could learn about the place and the people who hold these fascinating beliefs. Luckily, I have a friend and former student named Adrienne with a wicked droll wit who lived and practiced law in Salt Lake City at the time, so I invited her to join me at the group's pyramid with the promise that afterward we would stop by the Beerhive, a terrific place with a strip of ice embedded in the bar to keep your drinks cold, to discuss what we'd seen and learned. The class took place within the pyramid, which we were pretty psyched about; even better was how the door to the pyramid opens up and out like a DeLorean or the spaceship in *Close Encounters of the Third Kind.* We entered the pyramid along with several members of the Summum and two other people who might also have been members, though we weren't totally sure.[‡]

The inside of the pyramid was fantastic. Toward one side was an

---

[‡] It's hard to know exactly how many people would describe themselves as Summum believers. One lawyer who has represented the Summum told me that somewhere around six thousand people have made more than an initial communication with the group. I suspect, however, that the active membership is quite small. Maybe two dozen people? Eight people?

elaborate display of mummified cats, a picture of Corky, two large vases with peacock feathers reaching up toward the twenty-seven-foot-high roof, a statue of the Buddha, and, behind all of these items, seemingly watching over them and everything else in the pyramid, the actual mummified remains of Corky in an elaborate and lovely sarcophagus. Su Menu, the current president of the Summum, a musician in her mid-sixties with long gray hair, wearing a light-colored jeans jacket and dark navy jeans, took a seat by the display, kind of right in front of Corky. To her right sat Ron Temu, another core member of the group, who, as a licensed funeral director, leads the group's mummification practice. The third core member, Bernie Aua, sat on the other side of the pyramid behind some kind of an audiovisual board and prepared to videotape the session. Adrienne and I settled into a couch covered with a pyramid design to the left of Su, and the other two guys took seats in two of the remaining chairs. I had no idea what to expect.

Given how interesting the Summum are, and how cool the setting was, the "class" turned out to be surprisingly boring. It consisted simply of Su reading passages from Joseph Campbell's *The Hero with a Thousand Faces*. Once or twice, Su put the book down and either she or Ron riffed on something she had read, and those were the moments when the subject matter became interesting. For example, Su described Corky's first meeting with the Summum; his visit to the pyramid, she said, was "not a dream" but a real trip, and he really did walk through the walls of the pyramid to find the Summum inside. Besides those few comments, though, what I mostly focused on was gazing around the inside of the pyramid so I could remember what it looked like. I counted the mummified cats several times. So did Adrienne. When we adjourned to the Beerhive after the class, we compared notes. I had counted ten, but she had counted eleven. Probably she was right. She also noticed a couple of other things that I had overlooked. For instance, I had seen the stuffed frog and the two teddy bears that were on a shelf on one of the pyramid's walls, but I had not noticed the plush snake with a plush mouse on top of it in front of the cats, which had caught Adrienne's attention (she thought it might have been some sort of offering to the cats), or the mummified rat, which she conceded might have just been a stuffed animal with green tape wrapped around it.

When the class ended, I asked Su about the cats. She had just finished reading a long passage about the importance of religious symbols, so I was curious as to whether they had any special meaning.

"What is the significance of the cats to your faith?" I asked.

Su looked at me like I had asked her the craziest question of all time. "We just like cats," she said.

"Ah," I responded. "Got it."

As we were leaving, Ron gave Adrienne and me each a publication about the Summum for our reading pleasure. One was a short pamphlet that tells the story of Corky's first encounter with the Summum that one fateful day in the pyramid. The other document, however, was the real treasure. Titled *Sexual Ecstasy from Ancient Wisdom: The Joys of Permanent Sexual Ecstasy*, this was a wire-bound sixty-page fully illustrated, completely explicit text about, well, how to achieve sexual ecstasy. The book came seemingly out of nowhere—nothing in the class or the setting or anything we had talked about with the Summum thus far had anything to do with sex, much less permanent sexual ecstasy. Ron explained that this was the Summum's basic religious text, and the book's introduction links the group's religious beliefs to the sexual instructions (and explicit pictures) in the rest of the text:

> The basic knowledge of the sexual principles introduced in this text is found in the esoteric teachings of every ancient culture. Even the most ancient sexual teachings of India and Egypt have their roots in these principles. At the source of this knowledge are the Summa Individuals, beings who come to this planet to assist in the teaching of the mysteries, joys and delights of the ancient sexual wisdom; and who, throughout time, have taught and enlightened advanced teachers from all areas of this planet.

The book's teachings are pretty straightforward and nothing really that you couldn't find in something like *The Joy of Sex* or a basic on-line how-to manual. The one exception is the description of a "luxurious oil based lubricant formulated from ancient wisdom" called "MERH," which would seem to be an absolutely necessary element of any top-notch sex life. As the book explains, "The consistency of MERH comes from a blend which provides the greatest sensitivity and a perfect lubricant for prolonged sexual ecstasy. Generous use of MERH is suggested so that your entire genital area is completely and liberally covered with MERH. Water based jellies and other lotions or creams will in no way allow you to experience prolonged sexual ecstasy the way MERH will. You will find no substitute that can maintain the milieu necessary for this total experience." I looked online afterward and found that you can buy an eight-ounce jar of MERH from the Summum for fifteen dollars, but if you do that, make sure to heed the warning provided in the *Sexual Ecstasy* booklet: "Please note that cats are extremely attracted to MERH and will eat the MERH directly from the container, preferring it over even their favorite delicacy."

We just like cats.

* * *

Before Adrienne arrived, I had the chance to talk to Su, Ron, and Bernie about the Summum's unsuccessful quest to get the town of Pleasant Grove to put up a Seven Aphorisms monument next to the Ten Commandments in Pioneer Park. The idea had been Corky's. According to Su, he saw the Ten Commandments monument in the park and thought, "If they can do it, then why not us?" There has never been an actual Seven Aphorisms monument; unlike the Satanic Temple's veterans monument, the Summum's monument has never made it past an artist's rendering. I asked the group whether the goal of the monument was to gain new followers to the faith, and the answer was a resounding no. "We don't proselytize. When people are ready, they'll find us," Ron answered. Bernie elaborated: "To me, Corky is like Jesus or Buddha. He wanted to teach others a good way of living and wasn't trying to start a thing." I asked whether people ended up learning about the Summum as a result of the group's efforts to get the monument put up. "People learned about the faith. A lot came around and were curious," Ron told me. "There's a lot to learn about the Summum. They learned about our principles. To a point." Later on, when I met with Stewart Gollan, one of the Summum's attorneys, and asked him the same thing, he told me that the controversy "raised consciousness about the existence of the group, but not its substance."

Would more people have learned about the Summum if Pleasant Grove had allowed the group to put up a Seven Aphorisms monument next to the

Ten Commandments monument in Pioneer Park? It seems likely, but sadly, we will never know, because the town refused to install it on the grounds that it had nothing to do with the history of the town and was not donated by a group with strong ties to the community. Both the U.S. Supreme Court and the Utah Supreme Court upheld the town's decision.

The U.S. Supreme Court's decision was unanimous, fairly straight-forward, and almost certainly correct. The key to the decision was that there is an important distinction in constitutional law between government speech and private speech. The government is limited by the Free Speech Clause of the First Amendment ("Congress shall make no law . . . abridg-ing the freedom of speech") when it comes to regulating private speech, but when it comes to its own speech, the government can basically say whatever it wants, subject really only to the Establishment Clause, which prohibits the government from endorsing religion and which was not at issue in the *Summum* case. When the government erects a monument, it is generally speaking for itself, expressing its own views and ideals, and that means that nobody has the right to demand that the government erect monuments with different or contrary messages. As Justice Alito's opinion explained, the alternative would be unworkable and basically crazy: "Every jurisdiction that has accepted a donated war memorial may be asked to provide equal treatment for a donated monument questioning the cause for which the veterans fought. New York City, having accepted a donated statue of one heroic dog (Balto, the sled dog who brought medicine to Nome, Alaska, during a diphtheria epidemic) may be pressed to accept monuments for other dogs who are claimed to be equally worthy of com-memoration." This makes perfect sense. Imagine if the government, having put up a monument to women's equality, were forced to erect a monu-ment to male supremacy next to it, or if every monument proclaiming the glories of human liberty had to be accompanied by one that celebrates bondage and slavery?

In the wake of the Supreme Court's decision, the Summum took its case to the Utah court system, challenging the town's actions as violat-ing article I, section 4 of the Utah Constitution, which, like many state constitutions, prohibits the use of public money or property for "religious worship, exercise or instruction." The problem was that the Summum was not challenging the placement of the Ten Commandments monument in the park—indeed, as Su and Ron told me when I talked to them in Salt Lake, the Summum believes in the Ten Commandments and didn't want them to come down. Since there's really no plausible argument that the clause in the Utah Constitution relied upon by the Summum requires the government to put up *more* religious monuments, the Utah Supreme Court quickly disposed of the case.§

* * *

If all this seems unpalatable from the perspective of religious minorities and nonbelievers who would like to participate in public life by insisting that towns erect their monuments on public property, it is. Under normal circumstances, a city or town has no obligation to approve a request by anyone to put up a monument on its property. Moreover, such a city or town *can* have a monument of the Ten Commandments on its land, at least if that monument has been around a long time and is surrounded by other monuments. The Court's decision in *Summum* may seem unjust, but it's important to recognize that the real problem is with *Van Orden*, not *Summum*. In other words, the problem is not that the government can refuse to install someone's religious monument but rather than it *can* put up a monument to the Ten Commandments, which, contrary to the blathering of Justice Breyer and his brethren who agreed with him, does in fact undoubtedly endorse a particular religious belief, in violation of the Constitution.

All, however, is not lost. For one thing, *Van Orden* is limited to its specific facts, at least for now. Just because the government can keep a Ten Commandments monument on its property if it's been there for forty years does not mean, of course, that it can install a brand-new one, particularly

---

§   To complete the story, the Summum also brought a weird Establishment Clause claim in federal district court after it lost in the U.S. Supreme Court. Weird for the same reason that its challenge brought under the Utah Constitution was strange--it wasn't really seeking the removal of the Ten Commandments monument. Still, though, the district court observed that the Ten Commandments monument in Pioneer Park was basically just like the Texas monument that was at issue in *Van Orden v. Perry* and said that it did not violate the First Amendment.

if it is not part of a larger collection of monuments. Second, and more important, if the government allows individuals or groups to put up private monuments or displays or symbols as part of what is known as a public forum—in other words, if the government decides to facilitate *private* speech as opposed to speaking for itself—then it cannot exclude religious minorities or secular points of view from participation in that forum without violating the Constitution. This rule, which I discuss in chapter 2, has proven to be a powerful tool for religious minorities and others who wish to participate in public life alongside our Christian majority.

2

PAGANS, PENTACLES,
AND PLURALISM

Religious Displays in the Public Forum

IN LATE SEPTEMBER 2005, Sergeant Patrick Stewart of the Nevada National Guard was killed in Afghanistan when the Chinook helicopter he was flying in was shot down by Al Qaeda forces. Sergeant Stewart, who had also served in Operation Iraqi Freedom, was—as his military identification tags made clear—a practicing Wiccan. A large number of Wiccans serve in the U.S. armed forces, so his wife, Roberta Stewart, was both surprised and upset when she learned that the Wiccan pentacle—a five-pointed star surrounded by a circle—was not on the list of symbols approved by the Department of Veterans Affairs (VA) for placement on the gravestones of fallen soldiers. She could have gotten her husband's stone one of a dozen or so crosses, the Jewish Star of David, the Muslim Crescent and Star, a Buddhist Wheel of Righteousness, or even a Humanist Emblem of Spirit, but no Wiccan pentacle.

Stewart got on the phone with Selena Fox, a Wiccan priestess who runs the renowned Circle Sanctuary in southern Wisconsin, one of the largest Wiccan communities in the country. Fox, an experienced advocate for Wiccan rights, had been working with a number of Wiccan individuals and groups who had been trying since 1997 to get the VA to approve the pentacle symbol and had also filed an application on behalf of Circle Sanctuary and its members in 2005. The VA's response to these petitions and applications had been a mixture of silence and misdirection; several times the agency told applicants that it was working on changes to the process for adding symbols to its approved list, all the while approving, generally quickly and without much fuss, symbols other than the pentacle. In other words, the VA was clearly giving the Wiccans the runaround.

Even though Selena Fox had previously worked productively with the military on issues involving Wiccan chaplains, at first she had no more success than anyone else who had asked the VA to approve the Wiccan pentacle. After speaking directly with the under secretary of Veterans Affairs in charge of the cemetery marker program in Washington on numerous occasions over the course of several months, she became convinced that the various applications for recognition of the Wiccan pentacle that had been filed "were stuck in . . . bureaucratic limbo" and were "not being treated procedurally the same as applications by other groups." In the summer of 2006, Fox and Roberta Stewart met with lawyers from the separationist watchdog group Americans United for Separation of Church and State (AU). If the VA wouldn't voluntarily stop discriminating against Wiccans, then Fox and her allies would take the pentacle quest to the next level. In November, AU filed suit.

* * *

It is no easy task to describe the Wiccan religion. Wicca is a subset of Neo-Paganism, but that doesn't help much because it is even more difficult to describe Paganism than it is to describe Wicca. Paganism has no official structure or hierarchy or list of tenets; countless Pagan communities are scattered all over the United States, and some Pagans are members of no larger religious community at all. There may be as many as several hundred thousand people in the country who identify as Pagan, but nobody knows the number for sure. Many are environmentalists. Some believe in magic. Others trace their roots back to premodern traditions in various European states. Some integrate science fiction into their belief systems. Probably the best I can do in trying to characterize them is to quote from Margot Adler's classic history of

Paganism in America, *Drawing Down the Moon*, in which she attempts
to capture the essence of Pagan faith as found in this country:

> Most Neo-Pagans sense an aliveness and "presence" in nature. They are
> usually polytheists or animists or pantheists, or two or three of these
> things at once. They share the goal of living in harmony with nature and
> they tend to view humanity's "advancement" and separation from na-
> ture as the prime source of alienation. They see *ritual* as a tool to end
> that alienation. Most Neo-Pagans look to the old pre-Christian nature
> religions of Europe, the ecstatic religions, and the mystery traditions as
> a source of inspiration and nourishment. They gravitate to ancient sym-
> bols and ancient myths, to the old polytheistic religions of the Greeks,
> the Egyptians, the Celts, and the Sumerians. They are reclaiming these
> sources, transforming them into something new.

As for Wicca, the term itself is an Old English word meaning "witch,"
and most of the Wiccans whom I've met embrace the term (indeed, one
Wiccan told me that revealing oneself to the world as a Wiccan is known
as "coming out of the broom closet"). Wiccans bear little resemblance,
however, to the cackling, spell-casting, wart-speckled evildoers with the
pointy black hats of Halloween caricature. Some believe in magic, of
course, but not of the abracadabra sort; as Adler puts it, magic is more
like "the use of imaginative faculties, particularly the ability to visualize,
in order to begin to understand how other beings function in nature so
we can use this knowledge to achieve necessary ends."

There is a lot of disagreement and confusion among Wiccans about the
history of Wicca, but many trace it back to the writings of a nudist Brit
named Gerald Gardner, who may or may not have been initiated into a
coven of witches that originated in premodern times and who published,
following the repeal of the Witchcraft Acts in 1951, a couple of books
that are considered by some to be the foundational texts of the tradition.
As with Paganism more generally, Wicca has no authoritative hierarchical
structure, so it's very difficult to generalize about the beliefs or practices
of the religion, but a couple of things seem fairly clear. Wiccans, according
to Adler, tend to "consider themselves priests and priestesses of an ancient

European shamanistic nature religion that worships a goddess who is related to the ancient Mother Goddess in her three aspects of Maiden, Mother, and Crone." Moreover, whatever other rituals and holidays Wiccans may celebrate, nearly all of them recognize the Celtic New Year of Samhain, which falls on October 31, and the fertility festival of Beltane, which is celebrated annually on May 1.

* * *

Although the Supreme Court has interpreted both the Free Exercise Clause of the First Amendment and the Equal Protection Clause of the Fourteenth Amendment as forbidding the government from discriminating against any particular religion, the most relevant constitutional provision for this chapter is really the Free Speech Clause of the First Amendment. That clause, of course, restricts how the government can regulate speech and expression, including religious speech and expression. As with the Establishment Clause, however, very little about the Free Speech Clause is straightforward.

When considering the Free Speech Clause, it is important to understand the distinction between what the Supreme Court calls "content-neutral" restrictions of speech and "content-based" restrictions of speech. A content-based restriction is one that targets either the subject matter or the viewpoint of the speech. So, for example, a law that prohibited anyone from speaking about the Holocaust in public would be a subject matter restriction, while a law that prohibited anyone from denying the existence of the Holocaust (some European countries have laws like this) would be a viewpoint restriction. Likewise, prohibiting speech about abortion would be a subject matter prohibition, while prohibiting speech that advocates pro-choice positions would be a viewpoint prohibition. Unlike content-based restrictions, content-neutral regulations do not target the expressive nature of the speech that is being regulated. These regulations are often referred to as "time, place, or manner" regulations. Examples might include laws that prohibit the use of bullhorns in public or restrict how many signs someone can put on his or her front lawn or refuse to allow protestors—regardless of what they're protesting—to use a park after dark.

The Supreme Court has always been very wary of content-based restrictions on speech or expression and has almost always invalidated them as violations of the First Amendment,* although, as we will see, the Court has reserved its most rigorous scrutiny for viewpoint, rather than subject matter, restrictions. Viewpoint restrictions are particularly dangerous because they allow the government to make debate about important issues completely one-sided. This is why, for example, the government cannot prohibit the burning or desecration of the American flag. Indeed, it was in the classic flag-burning case of *Texas v. Johnson* that Justice Brennan wrote the famous line that summarizes the Court's attitude toward viewpoint-based restrictions: "If there is a bedrock principle underlying the First Amendment, it is that the Government may not prohibit the expression of an idea simply because society finds the idea itself offensive or disagreeable." When it comes to content-neutral restrictions, however, the Court sometimes upholds these restrictions and sometimes does not, depending on a variety of factors, including whether the regulation, in the Court's view, restricts *too much* speech. As a general matter, the Court applies what is known as "intermediate scrutiny" to content-neutral regulations, which means that the government must show that its regulation furthers an important interest and does not cut off alternative channels of communication. Content-based regulations, on the other hand, receive "strict scrutiny," which requires the government to show that its regulation is narrowly tailored to achieve a compelling interest, something that is usually impossible to demonstrate.

As we saw in chapter 1, these rules do not apply to the government's own speech. The government itself can speak on any subject matter it wants to, and it can express whatever viewpoint it wants, subject only to the limits imposed by the Establishment Clause—i.e., it cannot endorse religion. When it comes to regulating *private* speech on government property,

---

* There are, as with any area of constitutional law, exceptions. In the free speech area, for example, the Court has carved out certain categories of speech that are treated differently from speech generally, such as obscene speech or libelous speech. For instance, the Court has held unequivocally that the government may prohibit child pornography, even though, of course, such a prohibition is a content-based restriction on speech.

however, the rules about content-neutral and content-based restrictions on speech do apply, although in a specialized and fairly complicated way. Here we have to delve into the murky world of what the Court refers to as its "public forum doctrine." If it turns out that after reading the next couple of paragraphs about this doctrine you're still a little confused about it, don't worry, because you will share that confusion with roughly everybody else who has ever studied it (including me).

To begin with, the Court has recognized the existence of what it calls "traditional public fora," places like public streets and parks, which "have immemorially been held in trust for the use of the public and, time out of mind, have been used for purposes of assembly, communicating thoughts between citizens, and discussing public questions." In public fora, the traditional rules about content-neutral and content-based regulations apply—reasonable time, place, or manner restrictions may be okay, but content-based restrictions must meet strict scrutiny and are therefore almost always not okay. Then there are places that have traditionally not been open for free public communication. In these "non-public fora" like army bases, the interior of courtrooms, government offices, and the like, the government has much more authority to regulate and restrict speech. It can, as the Court has said, "reserve the forum for its intended purposes, communicative or otherwise, as long as the regulation on speech is reasonable and not an effort to suppress expression merely because public officials oppose the speaker's view."

Finally, the government can voluntarily open up an area that has not been traditionally used for public communication to create a "designated public forum" for speech. For example, a town could announce that from January 1 to February 1 the foyer of its courthouse will be a public forum for communicative activity; if it does so, then presto, the courthouse foyer becomes a public forum for expression, and everyone can come in with signs and leaflets saying whatever they want. Once the government creates such a designated public forum, then it must treat the space like a true public forum, meaning that it can impose reasonable content-neutral restrictions but may not generally restrict speech within the forum on the basis of its content. The one exception—and it's potentially a very important exception—is that the state is entitled, if it so chooses, to create a forum that is limited to the "discussion of certain subjects." This is known as a "designated limited public forum." In such spaces, the government *can* restrict speech on the basis of its subject matter (e.g., speech in the courthouse foyer shall be limited to speech about the criminal justice system), but it still may not restrict speech on the basis of its viewpoint.[†]

The designated public forum is an extremely important legal concept when it comes to how religion can participate in public life. For one thing, as I'll discuss in a later chapter, it means that when a public school or university opens up its classrooms for use by student groups before and after school, thus creating a designated public forum in those classrooms, it may exclude a group on the basis of the subject matter of the club but not on the basis of the viewpoint that the club expresses, which raises the thorny question—bandied about by the Court on several occasions—of whether religion is a subject or a viewpoint. More relevant to the discussion here, however, is that when the government has opened up an area of its property to private religious expression, as opposed to using it for its own expression, then it may not discriminate on the basis of viewpoint, meaning that it must treat all religions equally. In other words, if the government says that religious groups can use a certain area of its property to express their religious viewpoints, and someone puts up a display of the Ten Commandments or a Nativity scene, then the government must also allow minority religious groups and even nonbelievers to put up their own displays, whether those happen to be a statue of the Buddha, a Hindu god, or a cross sponsored by the Ku Klux Klan.

Indeed, the one time that the Supreme Court specifically considered the issue of privately sponsored religious displays in a public forum, the precise question was whether the City of Columbus, Ohio, could prohibit

---

† It is not always clear whether the government has opened up a public forum or not. Take license plates, for instance. When a state creates a program that allows drivers to choose from a variety of plates with different messages—"We Love New Jersey," "I'd Rather Be Golfing," "Save the Whales," "Choose Life"—is it speaking for itself, or is it opening up a forum for private speech? Not an easy question. The Court in the 2015 case *Walker v. Texas Division, Sons of Confederate Veterans* held that the license plates in Texas's program were government speech, not private speech, and so the state could refuse a request to create a plate with the Confederate flag on it.

the Klan from erecting a cross in such a forum near the state capitol building. A state statute provided that the ten-acre state-owned plaza near the
capitol would be available "for use by the public . . . for free discussion of
public questions, or for activities of a broad public purpose." Any person
or group that wanted to install a display simply had to file an application, demonstrate that the display would be safe and sanitary, and meet a
few other content-neutral requirements. In November 1993, the Capitol
Square Review and Advisory Board approved the state's request to put
up a Christmas tree as well as the request of a local rabbi who wanted to
put up a menorah. The same day that the board approved the menorah, it
received an application from an officer of the Ohio Ku Klux Klan to put
up a cross for two weeks during December. The board denied the request,
stating that such a denial "is a good faith attempt to comply with the Ohio
and United States Constitutions, as they have been interpreted in relevant
decisions by the Federal and State Courts."

When the case made it to the Supreme Court, the board did not argue
that it could exclude the Klan's cross because it disagreed with the message of the display. That's because such an argument would have been
frivolous, as Justice Scalia, writing for the Court in *Capitol Square Review
and Advisory Board v. Pinette*, explained:

> Respondents' religious display in Capitol Square was private expression.
> Our precedent establishes that private religious speech, far from being a First
> Amendment orphan, is as fully protected under the Free Speech Clause as
> secular private expression. . . . The right to use government property for one's
> private expression depends upon whether the property has by law or tradi-
> tion been given the status of a public forum, or rather has been reserved for
> specific official uses. If the former, a State's right to limit protected expressive
> activity is sharply circumscribed: It may impose reasonable, content-neutral
> time, place, and manner restrictions (a ban on all unattended displays, which
> did not exist here, might be one such), but it may regulate expressive *con-
> tent* only if such a restriction is necessary, and narrowly drawn, to serve a
> compelling state interest. These strict standards apply here, since the [lower
> courts] found that Capitol Square was a traditional public forum.

With this argument being a non-starter, the board's primary contention in the case was that it had to prohibit the Klan from putting up its cross because, given the proximity of the cross to the capitol, reasonable observers might wrongly believe the city was endorsing the Klan's message in violation of the Establishment Clause. That argument, if successful, would likely have had a significant limiting impact on the government's authority to create a public forum for the placement of private religious symbols anywhere near government buildings or other official government landmarks.

Ultimately, though, the argument was not successful. Although several justices had at least some sympathy with the board's view, the majority held that so long as the government has truly opened up a public forum for private religious speech, that speech cannot itself violate the Establishment Clause simply because some passerby might get confused and think that it's the government speaking rather than a private party. As the Court's concluding sentence stated: "Religious expression cannot violate the Establishment Clause where it (1) is purely private and (2) occurs in a traditional or designated public forum, publicly announced and open to all on equal terms. Those conditions are satisfied here." The city, in other words, was not allowed to prohibit the Klan from putting up its cross.

* * *

Over the past decade, religious minorities and Atheists have often sought to take advantage of the Court's rulings on speech in the public forum by demanding that they be allowed to put up their own displays alongside Christian ones. Some of these attempts have gone relatively smoothly; others not so much.

Atheist groups have probably been the most active, aggressive, and successful of all non-Christians in getting their displays placed in public spaces. When the Community Men's Fellowship erected a Ten Commandments monument in front of the courthouse in Bradford County, Florida, for example, a group called the American Atheists, founded by famous Atheist Madalyn Murray O'Hair in the 1960s and known for the controversial anti-religious billboards that it regularly displays on the sides of highways across the country,[‡] sued to have the monument removed. While the case was in mediation, the conservative northern Florida county offered to let the Atheist group put up its own monument. The American Atheists decided they liked the idea and, with a grant from the Stiefel Freethought Foundation, paid local masons to build a 1,500-pound granite bench and engrave it with quotes from O'Hair, Benjamin Franklin, and Thomas Jefferson. One of those quotes—the one from O'Hair—reads: "An atheist believes that a hospital should be built instead of a church. An atheist believes that deed must be done instead of prayer. An atheist strives for involvement in life and not escape into death. He wants disease conquered, poverty banished, war eliminated." Also engraved on the bench was a list of punishments from the Old Testament for violating the Ten Commandments, including stoning. American Atheists wanted the monument to take the form of a bench, according to David Silverman, the organization's president, so it would have a "function" because "atheists are about the real and the physical."

The monument was revealed in July 2013 and as of September 2018 was still standing. The unveiling ceremony was mostly, though not entirely, without incident. Groups of protestors apparently played Christian country music and waved signs that read, "Honk for Jesus" and "Yankees Go Home." Someone driving past in a car threw a toilet seat (!) out of the car window at the crowd but missed. According to the *New York Daily News*, one protestor complained, "It's a stick in the eye to the Christian people of Florida to have these outsiders come down here with their money and their leadership and promote their outside values here." Most of the two hundred or so people who were present at the ceremony, however, were supportive, or at least respectfully quiet, and no small number of them were eager to have their picture taken with the groundbreaking monument.

---

‡ In 2016, for instance, the group put up two different billboards in five locations, mostly in the South. One billboard read "MAKE CHRISTMAS GREAT AGAIN: Skip Church!" while the second one proclaimed: "Atheist Christmas: The More the Merrier" and featured a text-message conversation between a teenager and her friend: "U going to church this Xmas" "LOL. No way. I don't believe that stuff anymore." "What'll your parents say?" "They'll get over it :--P"

The Freedom from Religion Foundation has also had success (often-times hard-won) in getting its Atheist messages into public parks and buildings. In 2016, for instance, the group persuaded the state of Iowa to allow it to install its "no religion nativity scene" in the capitol rotunda near a traditional Christian Nativity scene. FFRF's exhibit, a cutout depicting Benjamin Franklin, Thomas Jefferson, George Washington, and the Statue of Liberty looking lovingly down at a baby Bill of Rights with a sign proclaiming "Keep religion and government separate," stood without incident for about ten days during the Christmas season. Similarly, members of the organization have successfully lobbied for the right to erect holiday season exhibits in places like Hastings-on-Hudson, New York (a banner proclaiming "Reasons Greetings"), Wilkes-Barre, Pennsylvania (a banner proclaiming "Heathen's Greetings"), and the capitol grounds in both Washington and California (same cutout as in Iowa).

Of course, not all attempts to get Atheist messages displayed go smoothly. Consider what happened in Shelton, a small town in southwestern Connecticut whose most famous son is, from what I can tell, a backup quarterback with the Detroit Lions. When the town mounted a sparkling display of "Heralding Angels" in the community's Constitution Park, an FFRF member named Jerome Bloom sought permission from the town to display a banner declaring: "At this season of the Winter Solstice, LET REASON PREVAIL. There are no gods, no devils, no angels, no heaven or hell. There is only our natural world. Religion is but myth & superstition that hardens hearts & enslaves minds." When the town refused, FFRF sued. The town subsequently allowed Bloom to place the banner in a different park next to the community's own "Merry Christmas and Happy Holidays" sign, but a few days before Christmas somebody ripped a giant hole in Bloom's sign. As of this writing, there is still a $2,500 reward being offered for information leading to the arrest and prosecution of the perpetrator.

Other Atheist and Humanist groups have been even more creative in their efforts to occupy the public square alongside Christians. In 2003, Atheist groups in Lincoln, Nebraska, for instance, installed a "Tree of Knowledge" in the state's capitol rotunda alongside a Nativity scene sponsored by the Thomas More Society; instead of tinsel and angel figurines, the tree was adorned with pictures of prominent Atheists and quotes from figures like Thomas Jefferson and Carl Sagan. At the Chester County Courthouse in Philadelphia, renowned activist Margaret Downey and her Freethought Society erected a similar display festooned with books promoting secularism, managing to do so several times before the county closed down its public forum so it could control the content there.

In Florida, Atheist rabble-rouser Chaz Stevens regularly installs Festivus poles on government property, even inside the state capitol building. These six-foot poles, which Stevens makes out of Pabst Blue Ribbon cans, celebrate the holiday created by the father of *Seinfeld* writer Dan O'Keefe, who brought the idea to the world's attention in "The Strike," an episode of the series that he wrote. The holiday is intended to be an alternative to the commercialization of Christmas and includes such rituals as the "Airing of Grievances," in which everyone at the Festivus dinner table takes a turn letting everyone else know how they have disappointed them over the previous year. In 2016, Stevens put up a slightly different version of the pole in a public park in Deerfield Beach to protest Donald Trump's election victory. The "Distresstivus pole" is a bit shorter than the regular Festivus pole ("a shout-out to Donald's tiny hands"), comes wrapped in an upside-down American flag, is topped with a red "Make America Great Again" hat, and is "fastened all together with a big ol' safety pin."

In 2011, Atheists in Leesburg, Virginia, installed seven secular displays on the grounds of the Loudon County Courthouse next to a Nativity scene, including a mannequin of Luke Skywalker, a Church of the Flying Spaghetti Monster banner depicting the Virgin Mary holding some sort of noodle-and-meatball figure, and a skeleton Santa Claus on a cross. The displays caused quite the controversy in the area. Some religious residents argued that they were "outrageous" and "mean-spirited." Atheists countered that they were free to express themselves however they wanted. Objectors tore down the skeleton Santa not once but twice.

Atheists are not the only ones who have created controversy by insisting on constructing displays in a public forum. Enter once again the Wiccans. Back in 2007, both the mayor of Green Bay, Wisconsin, and the president of the city council invited representatives of non-Christian religions to submit contributions to an interfaith display on the roof of the city hall.

On December 14, Selena Fox's Circle Sanctuary submitted a Yuletide Pagan wreath with a Wiccan pentacle in it, and city officials placed the wreath next to the Nativity scene that was already on the roof. According to Fox, whose motto on these matters is "Many, if Any," she sent the wreath because "if there are to be holiday displays with religious symbols on public buildings and property, those displays need to accommodate America's religious pluralism." Three days later, someone went up to the roof, removed the Wiccan display, destroyed it, and left it behind some nearby shrubs. For a couple of days the city debated what to do next—resume the policy of accepting minority displays, take down all religious displays, or just let the Christian Nativity scene stand by itself. Rather than voting for either neutrality or pluralism, the city council voted in favor of the third option. The Freedom from Religion Foundation sued the city, but a court threw out the complaint on technical grounds. Nonetheless, the story ends sort of happily, as the following year the city decided to display only secular symbols at city hall, and nary a crèche was in sight.

* * *

What is a pentacle exactly? I mean, I knew that a pentacle is a five-pointed star (a pentagram) surrounded by a circle, but I didn't really understand what it meant or why the Wiccans fought so hard to have it on their veterans' headstones. Obviously I could have searched the Internet for answers, but I thought it would be better to go right to the source. I got in touch with Selena Fox at Circle Sanctuary and asked if I could come to Wisconsin to find out more. Selena could not have been more accommodating. She invited me to come out on Veterans Day, when, among other things, she would be conducting an evening class in the history, meaning, and use of the pentacle. Bingo!

The class met in the barn that serves as the office and base of Circle Sanctuary, which is located on two hundred beautiful wooded acres about forty-five minutes west of Madison. The group of ten or so sat in a circle, ready to learn about pentacles. The online class announcement had invited guests to bring a pentacle from home, so the table in the middle of our circle was covered with pentacles of different shapes and sizes— one engraved on a green bowl, another hanging from a pendant, a third handmade from wood. We soon turned our attention to Selena, a woman in her mid-sixties, with long, flowing gray hair. According to Wikipedia, she is "a Wiccan priestess, interfaith minister, environmentalist, pagan elder, author, and lecturer in the fields of pagan studies, ecopsychology, and comparative religion." The description is accurate. Over the course of the day that I spent at the sanctuary, I probably encountered her in all of these roles as she moved seamlessly from practitioner and scholar to advocate and observer. She's been in the nature game for a long time; among her accomplishments is helping to organize the first Earth Day, back in 1970. In the early 1980s, after more than ten years of practicing and speaking about Paganism, she started Circle Sanctuary and soon became perhaps the most public face and voice of modern Paganism in the United States. If anyone would know about pentacles, it was Selena.

"Tonight, we will take a journey to the realm of pentacles!" Selena announced, and the class began. After we went around the circle and one by one said what we hoped to learn from the class, Selena launched into a fairly comprehensive history of the use of five-pointed stars in a variety of ancient civilizations, from Mesopotamia, where apparently pentacles dating back six thousand years have been found, through Egypt, Sumeria, ancient Greece (where followers of Pythagoras would wear pentacle emblems to identify themselves), and Rome. As Christianity spread, the pentacle was sometimes appropriated to take on specifically Christian meanings—for instance, with the five points representing the five wounds of Christ. Selena took us through the Middle Ages, explained the use of pentacles in Zoroastrianism and Kabbalah Judaism, and brought us into the modern day, dropping references to the barn stars of the Pennsylvania Dutch, tarot cards, and the 1960s rock band Pentangle, which took its name from the figure on the knight Gawain's shield in the poem *Sir Gawain and the Green Knight*.

From history, Selena turned to meaning—specifically, the meaning of the pentacle to most Pagans. Each point represents one of the five elements (earth, air, water, fire, spirit), which in turn represent the different aspects of each human being (physical body, intellect, emotions, will, soul). The circle that connects the five points "represents being in harmony with the larger circle of nature of which we are a part." As a whole, the symbol signifies balance, well-being, healing, and protection. In some, but not all, Pagan traditions the pentacle is used to connect to the earth and the physical body. Selena explained that she sometimes puts sand or salt in a pentacle dish and then sprinkles it around her house as part of her own practice. The point about different Pagan traditions using or conceiving of the pentacle in different ways is an important one that she stressed several times during the evening. For example, traditions differ on where to start drawing the pentacle and how it should go from there. Some traditions interlace the lines of the pentacle, so it's possible to see where one line goes either under or over another line, while other traditions do not. Among the traditions that interlace, not all of them interlace in the same fashion.

How do Pagans *use* the pentacle as part of their rituals and everyday lives? That was Selena's next topic, and this time the class got participatory. For about five minutes, she led the group in a guided meditation during which we were asked to "imagine you are going to connect with the power of the pentacle in different colors and different traditions." I like meditating, so even though I don't personally have any special feelings for the pentacle, I gave it my best. It was relaxing and kind of fun to imagine that I was looking at a large green pentacle to my north and then a yellow one to the east and a red one to the south and so on, but I pretty much failed when I was supposed to let my "essence go right into the center" so I could "experience the spinning pentacle as the axis of the forces in harmony." When the meditation was over, we were all invited to choose one of the pentacle objects from the center of the table and to think about how we could use it, or what meaning it had for us. Then we were to share our thoughts with the group. I picked up a pretty blue platter with a white pentacle engraved in it and stared at it for a couple of minutes. When it was my turn to speak, I mumbled a bunch of nonsense, which fortunately I recorded and so am now able to report verbatim here:

> It's kind of uhh, uhh, I don't know how to describe it because the, the, the part that's up, like in relief, is, uhh, not the . . . uhh . . . ch/ch/ch part [here I draw a pentacle in the air with my finger] so you can look at it as, uhh, one way to look at it is as a pentagon and then five triangles then you can look at it the other way, where it's the ch/ch/ch [again with the finger drawing]. I keep going back and forth.

Luckily, Selena was charitable and used my yammering as a springboard for mentioning that the pentacle can be used as a "meditation object, like a Mandala, to transport ourselves to a different space and consciousness." Finally, after discussing how some Pagans like to bless their homes by drawing pentacles with their fingers on all the windows and others like to "walk a pentacle," particularly on a sandy beach where they can then see the shape they've made, we spread out and spent a couple of minutes all standing with our arms and legs extended like "living pentacles." That was fun too, although when I got back home and showed my wife how I could be a human pentacle, she shook her head and told me that I looked like Patrick, the starfish from *SpongeBob SquarePants*.

* * *

Around the same time that Americans United sued the VA to get the pentacle on the list of approved symbols at national cemeteries, Selena Fox and her fellow Wiccans at Circle Sanctuary launched the "Order of the Pentacle," an association of Pagan and Wiccan veterans and active-duty military personnel who hoped to someday have a Wiccan pentacle on their tombstones. The night of the pentacle class happened to be the tenth anniversary of the forming of the order, so Selena talked a little bit about the group, explaining that she had founded it "to bring attention to the quest and the cause" and that "as a result, people were finding out not just about pentacles but also about Wiccan spirituality and contemporary Paganism." She explained that whenever she spoke at rallies or press events during that time, she would make a point of wearing a large red-and-white pentacle, usually against a backdrop of blue clothes, in order to show that "we are Americans, and we deserve to have our symbol treated the same as other symbols."

It took Americans United less than six months to get the VA to cave and agree to the Wiccans' demands. The AU litigation group is small but highly talented. One of the primary lawyers on the pentacle case back in 2006 was Richard Katskee, a brilliant Yale-trained attorney who became the AU legal director in 2015. I've known Richard for quite a while, so when I was in Washington, DC, for some reason or other, I stopped by the AU offices and chatted with him about the case.

I hope it is fairly clear from what I've said so far that the Wiccans had a strong case against the VA. Remember the legal rules: If the government itself is speaking, it can say whatever it wants so long as it doesn't endorse religion, but if the government is instead opening a forum for private speech, then it cannot discriminate on the basis of viewpoint—e.g., allowing some religious symbols but not others. The question is whether the messages on the headstones in a national cemetery constitute government speech or private speech. Maybe if the government required that every single headstone contain the identical patriotic saying and nothing else (except for name, rank, and date, perhaps), then a plausible argument could be made that the gravestones were more government speech than private speech. But since the government has long allowed veterans and their families to choose from a large set of religious and non-religious symbols to have engraved on their headstones (at the time of the Wiccan lawsuit, there were thirty-eight symbols available), it seems pretty straightforward that the headstones contain private speech rather than government speech. Therefore, the VA had no right whatsoever to limit on the basis of content what kinds of religious or non-religious symbols a veteran could choose to display on his or her headstone.

Saying that their case is strong in theory, however, is not at all the same thing as saying that the Wiccans would necessarily have an easy time winning it. Litigation is no picnic, and so Fox and Stewart's decision to enlist Katskee and the crack AU team was a wise move. One of the early phases of a lawsuit is known as "discovery," during which each side hands over documents requested by the other side. When AU requested documents related to the Wiccan pentacle issue from the VA, the agency sent over what Katskee told me were roughly "a gazillion" pages. Lawyers at AU pored over thirty-plus boxes of stuff in their cramped DC offices, searching for anything in the document dump that could be used against the VA, and apparently they found some promising material. AU agreed as part of its settlement with the government not to copy or otherwise release too much of the content of the documents, so we don't know a lot about what these memos or e-mail messages said, but we do know that they revealed, as AU's press release put it, "that the VA's refusal to recognize the Pentacle was motivated by bias toward the Wiccan faith."

Specifically, the documents referred to a discriminatory statement about Wiccans made by George W. Bush while he was running for president. Since

1997, a coven of Wiccans known as Fort Hood Open Circle has held rituals and celebrated holidays on the grounds of the military base in Central Texas. In March 1999, a photographer took pictures of the group practicing its Vernal Equinox rituals, and the *Austin-American Statesman* published them. Conservative Christian groups freaked out. Senator Bob Barr called for the military to stop allowing Wiccans to practice their religion, arguing that it "sets a dangerous precedent that could easily result in the practice of all sorts of bizarre practices being supported by the military under the rubric of 'religion'" and asking, "What's next? Will armored divisions be forced to travel with sacrificial animals for Satanic rituals?"[§] On the June 24, 1999, episode of *Good Morning America*, George Bush was asked what he thought about the Wiccan ritual taking place on military property. He responded: "I don't think witchcraft is a religion, and I wish the military would take another look at this and decide against it." According to Barry Lynn, AU's executive director, the documents revealed in discovery showed that "the president's wishes were interpreted at a pretty high level . . . [the decision not to approve the Pentacle] became a political judgment, not a constitutional one."

With documents like these in hand, AU was able to get the VA to settle in short order. The agency agreed to approve the pentacle as a symbol for national cemetery headstones and to grant all of the pending applications from those who had requested the symbol. It also paid AU more than $200,000 in legal fees. Pagans across the country were jubilant. A woman who had applied to get pentacles on the headstones of both her parents told the *Washington Post*: "I am ecstatic. It makes us equal in the eyes of the law again." Selena told me that "people remember where they were when they heard" about the victory. Pagan communities held celebrations across the country. On May 1, the first headstones with pentacles were placed—two at Arlington National Cemetery and two, including the one for Patrick Stewart, at the cemetery on the grounds of Circle Sanctuary. Many Pagans serving in the military came out of the "broom closet" and started practicing more openly. On the whole, it was a tremendous victory, not only for constitutional equality and religious freedom but also for Paganism and the Wiccan tradition, both of which gained attention

---

§   Selena Fox refers to her late-1990s battles with Bob Barr as "Barr Wars."

and visibility from the very public pentacle campaign. Writing in Circle Sanctuary's quarterly publication, *Circle Magazine*, not long after the victory, Selena Fox summarized her view of the quest's legacy:

> The Veteran Pentacle Quest victory is an important breakthrough for equal rights on behalf of Wiccans, Pagans, and other practitioners of Nature religion. In addition to finally getting the Pentacle on the VA's list and included on veteran grave markers, the Quest succeeded in bringing about greater understanding about the Wiccan religion and Paganism, both in the USA and around the world. The Quest success also illustrated the importance of guarding and upholding Constitutional freedoms. The Quest made visible . . . the large numbers of Wiccans and other Pagans who have served and are serving in the US military. . . . The widespread support for the Quest, and the greater understanding about Paganism, has resulted in some Pagans' wearing pentacles openly and being more visible about their Paganism in other ways. The Wiccan religion now is more frequently being named alongside Judaism, Islam, Christianity, Buddhism, and other world religions in media reports discussing religious liberty.

One quick postscript to this part of the story: Soon after the VA settled with the Pagans and AU, the agency changed its rules about authorizing new symbols on its headstones. Now basically any design is allowed, subject to a few content-neutral restrictions; the design, for instance, cannot be too large or too complex to be etched on a headstone. In the last ten years, the VA has approved about twenty-five new symbols, including an infinity sign and the Hammer of Thor. In early 2017, the agency approved the "Awen," a Druid symbol that represents flowing spirit or energy. Druids are a type of Pagan, and the wife of the fallen soldier who wanted the Awen on his gravestone was assisted in her quest by who else but Selena Fox and Circle Sanctuary?

*   *   *

Of course, I wanted to see some of the new Pentagon-approved Wiccan pentacles for myself. Richard Katskee hooked me up with a couple of super-friendly Wiccans from northern Virginia, David and Jeanet Ewing, who sent me a list of Wiccans who had pentacles on their grave markers in Arlington National Cemetery. The Ewings, along with a few other Wiccans, celebrate their fallen brethren every Memorial Day by going from marker to marker (there are eight of them at the time of this writing) and performing a brief ritual at each one. I wasn't lucky enough to be able to visit on Memorial Day, but I did get a chance to visit the cemetery myself one overcast Saturday in February and view five of the eight markers, including the four headstones (the rest are plaques in the mausoleum portion of the cemetery). It's pretty hard not to be filled with emotion when visiting the incredible grounds of Arlington no matter what the occasion, with the seemingly endless rows of gravestones, but this trip was even more powerful for me than other times I had visited. I stood in front of each headstone, feet sinking into the soft mud, and tried to think both of the service that these soldiers had given to their country and the struggle, unnecessary as it should have been, that Roberta, Selena, and so many other Wiccans had to wage to get that very same country to recognize their faith.

I may have missed Memorial Day with the Ewings at the National Cemetery, but as I've already mentioned, I was fortunate enough to spend Veterans Day with Selena at Circle Sanctuary in southern Wisconsin. I arrived in midmorning at the house that Selena shares with her husband, who teaches at a nearby college and whom Selena describes as being "Pagnostic."¶ This was early November, so she still had all of her Halloween decorations up (for all I know, though, maybe she never takes them down)—what must have been hundreds of small witch and ghost and jack-o'-lantern figurines stared at us from around the kitchen and living room as we sat down and chatted about everything from her undergraduate days as a psychology major at the College of William & Mary to the recent election of Donald Trump.

Selena's life story is fascinating. Raised Southern Baptist in the 1950s, she grew up loving nature and having mystical experiences, although she

---

¶   The pentacle class that I described earlier actually took place at the end of the day, after Selena and her husband had not only graciously fed me lunch and dinner but also let me take a nap in their guest room. They are nice people.

didn't see these as being at odds with her Christian upbringing until high school. In college, it was a school project that convinced her she was Pagan; studying Latin but wanting to get more in touch with the classics than "reading Ovid over tea," she organized and carried out a spring ritual that "changed [her] life." After graduation, she enrolled as a Ph.D. student at Rutgers but left when it became clear that the psychology department there viewed her interest in studying the mind/body/sprit connection somewhat "strange." She had been engaged in social justice and environmental issues since her teenage years, and following her departure from Rutgers and arrival in southern Wisconsin in the early 1970s, she combined those interests with her Pagan beliefs and started Circle Sanctuary to serve both shortly thereafter.

I asked Selena whether the increased visibility enjoyed by Pagans over the past twenty-five years has improved the general public's understanding of Wiccans and other nature worshippers. Her answer was mixed. On the one hand, she agreed that more and more people have begun to appreciate Wiccan and Pagan traditions. On the other, though, she has witnessed a good deal of hostility toward individual Pagans and their communities. She mentioned examples of believers' being evicted from their homes or fired from their jobs for their beliefs. More broadly, she's seen anti-Pagan rallies, attempts by lawmakers (Orrin Hatch) to repeal tax-exempt status for Wiccans, and outright physical threats. Most bizarrely, she told me about her standoff in the early 1990s with Jeff Fenholt, a born-again evangelical Christian who had previously starred as Jesus in the original production of *Jesus Christ Superstar* and either was or was not a member (depending on whom you ask) of Ozzy Osbourne's classic heavy metal band Black Sabbath. Irrationally opposed to witches of all sorts, Fenholt announced his plans to invade Circle Sanctuary and confront Selena on the television show *The 700 Club* but was apparently dissuaded following through on his plan by the various restraining orders Selena obtained to keep him away. In talking about the threats to Pagan individuals and communities that continue to take place, Selena stressed to me that one of Circle Sanctuary's primary roles is to serve as a source of institutional support for Pagans of all stripes across the country who feel threatened by ignorance and cruelty.

After we had talked for a couple of hours, it was almost time for the Veterans Day proceedings to get under way, so Selena and I drove from her house to the barn that serves as the sanctuary's main offices and then hopped on her four-wheeler for the drive up to the sanctuary's very own cemetery. That's right: *Her four-wheeler*. In case you're wondering (and how could you not be?), the four-wheeler has a name, and its name is the Oakmobile. The tremendously weird and awesome scene was not lost on me. There I was, sitting next to Selena "Leadfoot" Fox, a famed Wiccan priestess, her long gray hair blowing in the wind as she zipped us at unsafe speeds up a steep hillside in her four-wheel off-road vehicle named the Oakmobile on our way to a Pagan Veterans Day celebration. I have to say that sometimes I really, really love my job.

The sanctuary's cemetery spans about twenty acres and includes both a traditional part and a "green cemetery" section, where Pagans who so desire can be buried directly in the ground without any embalming whatsoever. The ceremony took place at the summit of the hill in the more traditional part of the cemetery. It was a gorgeous fall day, crisp and windy, fallen leaves underfoot. We were joined by Selena's terrific assistant Ashley and two Pagan veterans, a Vietnam veteran known for patrolling the sanctuary's perimeter with a rifle to deter trespassers, and a somewhat younger transgender woman who interestingly had served at the very same base in Okinawa where the other vet had served some years earlier. Nine Wiccan veterans are buried in the cemetery, each with his own pentacle-graced headstone, including Patrick Stewart, whose headstone is located just a little bit apart from the rest. Selena gathered us and read a blessing, using a bowl and a bell and a little shaker for the appropriate sound effects, and then repeated the blessing in each of the four directions. She then blessed and thanked each of the nine buried veterans and said a little bit about each one of them. She ended with a final blessing, and then we all hugged. "We're huggers," one of the veterans told me.

After the ceremony, Selena and I got back into the Oakmobile for the ride home. First, though, she drove me around the sanctuary. It truly is a beautiful place. We passed near wide swaths of replanted prairie, a natural spring, and a maypole towering against the blue sky. We stopped by a small stream and got out to look around. Unfortunately, when we got back into the Oakmobile, the poor thing wouldn't start. Selena tried a few things to get it moving again, but soon declared it dead, at least for the moment (her husband got it started a little later in the day). We set out on foot and walked the rest of the way back to the barn.

* * *

The story of the Wiccan pentacle has a much happier ending than the story of the Summum Seven Aphorisms. The Summum were unable to either persuade or force the government to display the group's religious monument next to a Christian monument in a town park. The town did not want to endorse the religious views of the Summum by putting up the monument, and the Supreme Court, understandably, did not think the First Amendment should be read to require the government to endorse a message it did not believe in. As I've said before, the problem with the Summum scenario was not with the decision in *Summum* but rather the decision in *Van Orden*, which allowed the government to endorse the Ten Commandments, a clearly religious display. The difference between the Wiccan case and the Summum case turned on the different nature of the forum. Unlike the town park, which was neither a traditional nor a limited public forum, a national cemetery, at least with respect to the religious symbols allowed on headstones, is a limited public forum. As a result, the government cannot discriminate with respect to the content of the religious messages allowed on those headstones. Or rather, it can, and did, until a few brave and persistent individuals—Roberta Stewart, Selena Fox, and others—with the help of dedicated and talented legal counsel, forced the government to follow the law. Now the national cemeteries of the country are truly diverse when it comes to the religious symbols allowed on headstones—everything from a Wiccan pentacle to the Hammer of Thor to a Druid Awen to crosses and Jewish stars and all sorts of other symbols grace the memorial stones of our fallen soldiers. There is probably no more hopeful ending to a story in this book than the one I've tried to tell here.

It is worth noting that in this chapter I've focused on the concept of the public forum on government property in cases where there is a lot of space. When the plot of government land in question is big enough, the state will ordinarily not find it problematic to allow many different speakers with all kinds of opinions to make their views known within the public forum. But what if, theoretically, there was room for only one display in the public forum? For instance, what if the government opened up a two-foot-by-two-foot square of property for use by the public for its own expression? Would the first group to apply get to put up its display indefinitely in the space? Or would the government have to provide for a rotating series of displays—for instance, allowing each group to put up its display for a day, or a week, or whatever amount of time would seem appropriate? Of course, this is a bit of a silly example when it comes to erecting religious displays on public property, but think of a somewhat analogous situation: What if instead of talking about allowing private parties to erect displays on public property, we were talking about allowing private parties to give invocations or prayers before legislative sessions or town meetings? Assuming that only one person at a time can give an invocation, what obligation does the government have to allow people from diverse religious and non-religious traditions and backgrounds to take turns performing that function? That is the subject I turn to in chapter 3.

3

SECULARISM, STATEHOUSES, AND SCHOOL BOARDS

Prayers and Invocations before Government Bodies

UNLIKE ITS SOUTHERN EUROPEAN NAMESAKE, the town of Greece, New York, is known for neither its ancient philosophical figures nor its delicious salads.* The sleepy town of just under a hundred thousand residents is a fairly nondescript suburb of Rochester; until about the turn of the millennium, its biggest moment of fame was probably when brothers John and Walter Wegman founded Wegman's Food Market in the early 1930s. The town is run by a five-person board that meets monthly and makes decisions about zoning and parks and all other sorts of local business. Before 1999, the Greece Town Board, like many similar bodies across the country, began its meetings with a moment of silence.

In 1999, however, the town supervisor, a guy named John Auberger, decided that the town board would henceforth start each of its meetings with an actual prayer, given by a local member of the clergy. A town employee had the job of contacting all the religious organizations in town and asking if anyone there would want to pray at the town meeting. A list of people who were interested in doing so was compiled, and between

---

* Okay, I've basically stolen this joke from the hilarious comedian Gary Gulman, who has a bit about "what happened to the Greeks," but that's all right—we went to elementary school together and he said I could use it.

1999 and 2007, town employees would call the individuals on the list to schedule them to deliver the opening prayer. During this eight-year period, every single person invited to pray before the monthly town meeting was Christian.

Although about a third of the prayers were kind of generic (they referred not to Jesus, for example, but to the "Heavenly Father" or the "God of all creation"), the rest were thoroughly and explicitly Christian. According to a federal appeals court that was completely familiar with the record:

> Roughly two-thirds [of the prayers] contained references to "Jesus Christ," "Jesus," "Your Son," or the "Holy Spirit." Within this subset, almost all concluded with a statement that the prayer had been given in Jesus Christ's name. Typically, prayer-givers stated something like, "In Jesus's name we pray," or "We ask this in Christ's name." Some prayer-givers elaborated further, describing Christ as "our Savior," "God's only son," "the Lord," or part of the Holy Trinity. One prayer, for example, was given "in the name of the Lord and Savior Jesus Christ, who lives with you and the Holy Spirit, one God for ever and ever." Other prayers, including ones not expressly made in Christ's name, spoke of "the role of the Holy Spirit in our lives," and celebrated Christ's birth and resurrection.

Beginning sometime in 2001, a soft-spoken, civic-minded resident of Greece named Linda Stephens began attending the monthly town meeting in her capacity as a member of a town parks organization. Stephens is a longtime Atheist, and she found the town's practice of beginning each of its sessions with a Christian prayer to be highly irritating and offensive. In 2008, she and a fellow dissenter, a Jewish resident named Susan Galloway, began complaining to the town leaders about the prayer. In response, the town invited a couple of non-Christians to give the opening prayer, and in 2008 the invocation was delivered by a Wiccan priestess, the chairman of a local Baha'i congregation, and a Jewish layman. These minor exceptions to the Christian-only practice,† however, were

---

† Beginning in 2009, the town went back to the practice of inviting only Christians to give the opening prayer.

not sufficient for Stephens and Galloway, and so, with the help of AU, they sued, claiming that the town's practice violated the Establishment Clause of the First Amendment.

After Stephens and Galloway lost at the trial-court level, they took the case to the Second Circuit Court of Appeals in New York, and—to the surprise of many—they won. That court thought the relevant issue under the Establishment Clause was "whether the town's practice, viewed in its totality by an ordinary, reasonable observer, conveyed the view that the town favored or disfavored certain religious beliefs." Applying that test, the court held that Greece had in fact violated the Constitution, based on the way it chose who would give the prayers, the sectarian language in the prayers, and the fact that "most prayer-givers appeared to speak on behalf of the town and its residents, rather than on behalf of only themselves." On this last point, the court observed that many of the prayer-givers used first-person-plural language ("let us pray") and invited audience members to participate in the prayer by standing or bowing their heads.

Unfortunately, the plaintiffs' victory was short-lived. In a 5–4 decision written by Justice Kennedy, the Supreme Court reversed. I'll have quite a lot more to say about the opinions in the case of *Town of Greece v. Galloway* shortly, but for now I just want to flag the part of the opinion in which the Court said that the town may not discriminate on the basis of religion when it chooses who will give the opening prayer or invocation at its meetings. In other words, if a Buddhist or a Wiccan or a Jehovah's Witness asks to give the opening invocation at a meeting, the town cannot deny the request on the basis that it disagrees with the religious views of the applicant. It took about five minutes after the decision was issued for Atheists and members of minority faiths to start taking advantage of this part of the opinion. Americans United even set up something called "Operation Inclusion" to encourage non-Christians around the country to give invocations at all sorts of legislative and administrative sessions. Many Atheists took them up on the invitation.

One of those Atheists was none other than Linda Stephens, who asked the Town of Greece if she could give a secular invocation before the very board that she had previously sued. The town agreed, and Stephens's invocation was scheduled for October 2015. Would her invocation cause a holy hullabaloo in town? Would there be protests? Would she be shouted down? Burned in effigy? There was no way I was going to miss the opportunity to witness the occasion firsthand, so the day before the invocation was to take place, I boarded a plane and headed to Rochester.

* * *

The practice of opening a governmental meeting in the United States with a prayer goes back to the eighteenth century. Whenever someone says to me that we have a tradition of "separation of church and state" in this country, I like to remind that person (after I stop laughing) that both the House of Representatives and the U.S. Senate have had official chaplains on their payrolls since before the states ratified the Bill of Rights. As someone who has been studying and writing about church-state relations for almost twenty-five years, I have always found that fact to be bewildering. The most important government bodies in the nation have basically begun every session of business for almost the entirety of American history with a prayer. More like *shmeparation* of church and state, if you ask me.

The Supreme Court has considered the practice of praying before government bodies only twice. The first time was in 1983, when the Court upheld Nebraska's practice of starting every legislative session with a prayer given by a paid state chaplain. The case was called *Marsh v. Chambers*, and the Court's rationale was simply that a practice with such a long historical pedigree could not possibly violate the Establishment Clause. In my first book, I wrote that legal scholars generally agree that Justice Burger wrote his lackluster majority opinion in *Marsh* "in about five minutes while sitting on the can," but in retrospect I think this was inaccurate because there's no way he spent that long working on the decision. The dissent, written by Justice Brennan, explained how legislative prayers "violate the principles of neutrality and separation" protected by the First Amendment by injecting religion into politics, coercing nonbelievers into supporting belief systems with which they disagree and degrading religion, but the majority opinion had nothing to say about any of the objections.

When the Supreme Court finally returned to the issue thirty years later in *Town of Greece*, the facts differed from those in *Marsh* in several important ways. For one thing, in *Marsh*, although the state chaplain was Christian, he nonetheless stopped referring specifically to Christ after a Jewish legislator objected; in the *Town of Greece* case, however, most of the prayers contained explicit Christian references and imagery. The challengers in *Town of Greece* argued that although "non-sectarian" prayers might be acceptable, it should be a different story when the prayers were so clearly and overwhelmingly aligned with a specific faith.

Second, while *Marsh* involved a state legislature, *Town of Greece* involved a town board. The challengers argued that this was a critical distinction, not only because town board meetings are typically smaller and more intimate affairs where one is more likely to know other attendees than at a legislative session, but also because town boards often are asked to make decisions that directly affect the rights of specific individuals in the town. People come to town board meetings to request business licenses, zoning waivers, and all sorts of other things, and so, the argument went, in that setting an attendee might very well feel coerced to participate somehow in the prayer. Think about it. If you were a non-Christian attending a town board meeting at which the board was about to decide whether to allow you to operate a business, and the board opened the meeting with a Christian prayer, wouldn't you feel somewhat pressured to stand during the prayer or say "Amen" or otherwise give the prayer your "thumbs-up"? I know I would.

The Supreme Court's decision in *Town of Greece* was, to pretty much nobody's surprise, 5–4 in favor of the town. Justice Kennedy wrote the main opinion, and Justice Kagan wrote the primary dissent. In Justice Kennedy's view, the practice followed in Greece was not significantly different from the one the Court had upheld in *Marsh v. Chambers* and was therefore a constitutional recognition of the nation's religious history and identity. "By inviting ministers to serve as chaplain for the month, and welcoming them to the front of the room alongside civic leaders," Kennedy wrote, "the town is acknowledging the central place that religion, and religious institutions, hold in the lives of those present." The practice, according to the majority, is one that the framers of the Constitution clearly supported, as is evident from the fact that "the First Congress provided for the appointment of chaplains only days after approving language for the First Amendment."

From the perspective of the dissenters, however, the utterly sectarian nature of the prayers given in Greece, as well as the very different setting of the town board as compared to that of a state or national legislature, distinguished the case from *Marsh* and rendered Greece's practice unconstitutional. "[T]he Town of Greece should lose this case," Justice Kagan wrote. "[M]onth in and month out for over a decade, prayers steeped in only one faith, addressed toward members of the public, commenced meetings to discuss local affairs and distribute government benefits. In my view, that practice does not square with the First Amendment's promise that every citizen, irrespective of her religion, owns an equal share in her government." Kagan was particularly persuaded by the setting of the prayers. As she put it: "Greece's town meetings . . . revolve around ordinary members of the community. Each and every aspect of those sessions provides opportunities for Town residents to interact with public officials. And the most important parts enable those citizens to petition the government." On this point, Justice Kennedy was unconvinced. Perhaps, he mused, things would have been different if the record had shown that the town had treated citizens differently on the basis of how they responded to the prayer, but in his view the challengers had not shown "that town leaders allocated benefits and burdens based on participation in the prayer, or that citizens were received differently depending on whether they joined the invocation or quietly declined."

On the overtly sectarian nature of the prayers, Justice Kagan and the other dissenters thought that it is incumbent upon government bodies in our highly diverse religious society to make sure that those chosen to pray before their meetings speak in the most welcoming fashion possible. "When citizens of all faiths come to speak to each other and their elected representatives in a legislative session," Justice Kagan wrote, "the government must take especial care to ensure that the prayers they hear will seek to include, rather than serve to divide." Moreover, speaking "in nonsectarian terms, common to diverse religious groups," is hardly difficult, according to Kagan; "Priests and ministers, rabbis and imams give such invocations all the time." Justice Kennedy disagreed. In his view, requiring prayer-givers to speak in non-sectarian language not only would overly involve the government in religious affairs but also wouldn't solve the problem, since "[e]ven seemingly general references to God or the Father might alienate nonbelievers or polytheists." On this point, Justice Alito in a separate concurrence added that given the increasing religious diversity of the nation, including the growth of many Eastern religions, "composing a prayer that is acceptable to all members of the community who hold religious beliefs has become harder and harder." In sum, as Kennedy explained, "[o]nce it invites prayer into the public sphere, government must permit a prayer giver to address his or her own God or gods as conscience dictates, unfettered by what an administrator or judge considers to be nonsectarian."

In his separate dissent, Justice Breyer reiterated his view from *Van Orden* that only "legal judgment" and not any kind of judicially created "test" can distinguish constitutional from unconstitutional practices. For him, Greece's prayer practice fell on the unconstitutional side of the line, in large part because "the town made no significant effort to inform the area's non-Christian houses of worship about the possibility of delivering an opening prayer." Justice Alito responded to this argument by suggesting that "[t]he informal, imprecise way in which the town lined up guest chaplains is typical of the way in which many things are done in small and medium sized units of local governments." Kennedy agreed with Alito, noting that Greece had "made reasonable efforts to identify all of the congregations located within its borders and represented that it would welcome a prayer by any minister or layman who wished to give one." And then Kennedy added the line that is the most important one in the opinion for the purposes of this book: *"So long as the town maintains a policy of nondiscrimination, the Constitution does not require it to search beyond its borders for non-Christian prayer givers in an effort to achieve religious balancing."*

* * *

A few observations about the case are in order. First, note that nowhere in my description of what happened in the case did I mention the word "endorsement." None of the justices in the majority, in other words, were wondering whether the town board had sent a message to the people at the town meeting that Christians were the insiders and non-Christians the outsiders. That's because Justice Kennedy did not believe in the endorsement test, and so for him the only way the prayer practice was going to violate the Constitution was if it *coerced* nonbelievers into participating in religious activity. Unlike some of the other justices— notably Scalia and Thomas—Kennedy would likely have found coercion if he had really thought that the attendees experienced substantial psychological pressure to participate in the prayer,‡ but because they were typically adults, Kennedy was not worried about such a scenario. In his view, mature adults are quite capable of making their own decisions about whether to pray or not, and a dissenting adult of the Greece community had plenty of options—staying quiet, not standing, coming in late, leaving for the duration of the prayer—to avoid joining in the prayer.

I don't find Justice Kennedy's coercion analysis particularly persuasive, especially when it comes to people who have business before the board, but in my view his biggest mistake was looking for coercion, instead of endorsement, in the first place. The endorsement test, as I've said already, is hardly a perfect test, but it does appropriately render unconstitutional government efforts to symbolically promote religion over non-religion or particular religions over other religions. If it is unconstitutional for the government to put up a display of a crèche on public property because it endorses both religion generally and Christianity specifically, why doesn't it violate the Constitution for the government to engage in a prayer practice that does the same thing? In the Court's view, beginning a government meeting with a prayer "lends gravity to public business, reminds lawmakers to transcend petty differences in pursuit of a higher purpose, and expresses a common aspiration to a just and peaceful society." This may or may not be true from the perspective of someone who agrees with the

---

‡   Justices Thomas and Scalia have adhered to a force-based, *legal* coercion test to determine if a government-sponsored prayer is unconstitutional. This difference between Scalia and Kennedy is most visible in the 1992 case of *Lee v. Weisman*, which invalidated a public school's practice of inviting a member of the clergy to give a prayer at graduation. Kennedy found that the peer pressure likely felt by most students to stand and participate in the prayer was sufficient to make the practice unconstitutional. Justice Scalia thought that Justice Kennedy's position on this score was inane, and his angry, vitriolic dissenting opinion in the case stands as evidence of a man whose brain must have been on the brink of exploding.

prayer and its religious message, but from the point of view of someone who thinks the prayer-giver is talking about the wrong god or should be praying to more than one god, or who doesn't believe in any god at all, the notion is ludicrous. To that person, the prayer lends offensiveness to public business, reminds him or her that lawmakers are choosing to accentuate differences rather than to pursue a higher purpose, and expresses a divisive aspiration to a view of the world that they do not share. In my view, beginning a government meeting with a prayer is clearly an unconstitutional establishment of religion.

But wait, you might say—what about this "non-sectarian" point that the dissenters thought was so important? Couldn't the town simply tell the prayer-giver to keep his or her prayer general enough that it would speak to everyone? This brings me to my second observation about the case, which is that on this score Justice Kennedy and Justice Alito have it quite right when they question the very notion of such a prayer. The idea of a "non-sectarian" prayer is nonsense. Of course a general reference to "god" (much less to "the father"!) will alienate nonbelievers or polytheists. To believe otherwise is simply wishful thinking born in ignorance about what it means to be a nonbeliever or a polytheist. I don't really blame Justice Kagan and the dissenters for trying to find a compromise solution to this problem, and I agree that a prayer that speaks generically about "god" is probably a little better than one that talks about Jesus, but the fact is that there is simply no such thing as a prayer that will appeal to everyone. Now, why Justice Kennedy and the majority think that this is an argument *in favor of* divisive legislative prayer is beyond me—it seems quite clearly to be a slam-dunk argument *against* such a practice—but at least they don't rely on the notion that everyone can get behind a so-called nonsectarian prayer.

Third, and finally, there is the point about nondiscrimination. Justice Kennedy's opinion contains more than one statement indicating that when the government sponsors a practice of legislative prayer, it essentially creates a limited public forum in which anyone who wants to participate can do so by asking to give his or her own invocation. In addition to the "[s]o long as the town maintains a policy of nondiscrimination" sentence reported above, Justice Kennedy also wrote the following: "Adults often encounter speech they find disagreeable; and an Establishment Clause violation is not made out any time a person experiences a sense of affront from the expression of contrary religious views in a legislative forum, *especially where, as here, any member of the public is welcome in turn to offer an invocation reflecting his or her own convictions.*"§

Of course, since the town meeting is viewed as a limited public forum, as opposed to a traditional public forum, there are limits to what it must accommodate. For instance, Justice Kennedy's opinion suggests that a town might be able to restrict the forum to its own residents. It's also clear that a town can schedule speakers in a reasonable fashion; nobody has a right to insist on being able to give his or her invocation on a particular day or before a particular session. The most interesting and legally complicated limit that towns can presumably insist upon, however, has to do with the subject matter that the speaker wants to talk about. Clearly towns don't have to allow just any old speaker to get up and give an opening speech about any topic he or she might choose. A town resident who asked to start off a meeting with a three-minute "invocation" about his or her favorite football team or new business venture or opinions about health care policy would almost surely, and rightly, be denied by the town.

But how far does this discretion to deny speakers on the basis of what they might say extend? We know from Justice Kennedy's opinion that members of bona fide religious minorities must be allowed to give invocations, but again that begs the question of what counts as a bona fide religion, which is an incredibly difficult question to answer in the abstract. As a practical matter, usually it will be fairly clear whether or not someone fits within the spirit of Justice Kennedy's anti-discrimination principle, but in some cases, serious questions have already started popping up, including whether a town can prohibit an Atheist from giving

---

§   The italics are mine, not Justice Kennedy's. And while we're here in a footnote talking about Justice Kennedy, here's a little Justice Kennedy footnote trivia: Justice Kennedy never used footnotes. It's too bad. Everyone knows that footnotes are where the fun happens.

an invocation on the grounds that the subject matter of the limited public forum that the town has opened is restricted to religious belief and not its opposite.

* * *

In the wake of the Court's decision in *Town of Greece*, members of minority religious traditions stepped up their efforts to give invocations before legislative bodies and local town boards. Many of these occasions, thankfully, have proceeded without controversy or incident. But not all of them.

Take what happened in Huntsville, Alabama, to Wiccan Blake Kirk, for example. Before 2012, the Huntsville City Council had begun every meeting with a prayer given by a Christian minister. After FFRF threatened to sue, however, the city implemented a new system under which religious leaders from a variety of faiths were invited to give the opening invocation. Indeed, in September 2014, an Atheist gave the invocation in Huntsville, which was the first time such a thing had ever happened in Alabama. Blake Kirk's invocation, however, turned out to be more controversial than the Atheist's. Kirk was originally invited to give the opening prayer at the council's June 2014 meeting, but when the meeting agenda came out, announcing that Kirk was a priest of the "Oak, Ash and Thorn" tradition of Wicca, religious bigots flooded the city hall with angry phone calls and e-mail messages. In response, the city council revoked Kirk's invitation. As Kirk himself put it, "I guess somebody got the collywobbles." At that point AU intervened, writing a letter to the council and advising it that "if the City Council wishes to start its meetings with prayers, it must open the prayer opportunity to people of any and all religious beliefs—including Wiccans." The council quickly changed course and invited Kirk to open its November meeting. The invocation itself went smoothly, with most people in the audience reportedly bowing their heads. As AU pointed out in a subsequent press release, the city survived the prayer: "That's right—no tornadoes, earthquakes, meteors, or plagues of locusts have descended upon the community," AU wrote. "Everyone got through it."

A few months later, another controversy over a Wiccan invocation sprang up, this time in Iowa. When Deborah Maynard, a Cedar Rapids priestess, gave the opening prayer at the Iowa House of Representatives in April 2015,¶ more than half of the state's representatives weren't even there—they came to the meeting late specifically to miss the Pagan prayer. One representative, a Republican named Rob Taylor, did attend the prayer, but he turned his back during it, explaining afterward that he was just trying to do what Jesus would have done. Meanwhile, as Maynard was calling upon "spirit, which is ever present, to help us respect the interdependent web of all existence of which we are a part," several Christians in the audience were trying to counter the Wiccan blessing with prayers of their own. From the balcony, Pastor Michael Demastus, for instance, was, by his own words, "praying for Deborah Maynard . . . for her salvation . . . that she would come to know the one true God." Another woman in the audience told the *Cedar Rapids Gazette* that she had come to offer her own prayers in response to Maynard's because she didn't "want any demonic influences on the people who are making decisions on our behalf."

It will probably not be surprising to learn that Muslim invocations have also caused controversy around the country. When Republicans in the North Dakota House of Representatives learned that Nadim Koleilat, the president of Bismarck's Muslim Community Center, had been scheduled to give the opening prayer on Ash Wednesday in 2015, they canceled his invitation that morning. As Al Carlson, the House majority leader, put it, "Obviously we don't have any Muslims in this chamber." Koleilat instead switched positions with a Christian reverend who was scheduled to give the invocation in front of the state Senate across the hall and gave his invocation there. When the Minnesota chapter of the Council on American-Islamic Relations called for the House to issue an apology to Koleilat, Carlson refused, stating, "The consensus of the chamber is that

---

¶   According to the *Washington Post*, Maynard's invocation marked the third time a
Pagan had ever given the opening prayer at a statehouse session. The first occurred
in Oregon in 1999. The second took place in Wisconsin in 2009. Can you guess who
gave the Wisconsin invocation? If you didn't guess Selena Fox, you're wrong.

was the right thing to do on that day." Koleilat was instead invited to give the invocation later in the year.

Meanwhile, in Lincoln County, North Carolina, just northwest of Charlotte, a town commissioner named Carrol Mitchem made national news when he declared in May 2015 that prayers from minority religions should not be heard before county meetings. Mitchem had particularly strong words for Muslims. "I don't need no Arab or Muslim or whoever telling me what to do or us here in the country what to do about praying," he told a local newspaper. "If they don't like it, stay the hell away. . . . I ain't gonna have no new religion or pray to Allah or nothing like that." When a Muslim named Duston Barto gave the invocation before the county's board of commissioners meeting in August 2015, Mitchem left the room. Asked about his actions later, Mitchem said: "I said that I would not listen to a Muslim pray, is that not what I've said? I've done exactly what I said I was going to do. I'm not going to listen to them pray." At the end of the meeting, the board of commissioners voted 4–1, with only Mitchem dissenting, to scrap the county's invocation practice altogether and replace it with a moment of silence.

Lest you think that these incidents occur only in the southern and western parts of the country, consider the events of April 5, 2017, in Delaware. On that day, two Muslims gave the invocation before the Delaware Senate, quoting a passage of the Qur'an that calls for believers to "stand out firmly for justice." A Republican senator named Dave Lawson left the Senate chamber before the invocation, and upon his return gave a short speech to his colleagues in which he said: "We just heard from the Quran, which calls for our very demise. I fought for this country, not to be damned by someone that comes in here and prays to their God for our demise. I think that's despicable." Later in the day, the head of the Senate, Democrat David McBride, countered Lawson's hateful speech with a more welcoming message. "I am personally offended that our guests from the Muslim community and anyone else here in the chamber today would feel anything less than welcomed with open arms," he told the chamber. "[F]or our guests today to be branded as anti-American when our First Amendment of our country's Constitution explicitly guarantees the freedom of religion is both ironic and deeply sad to me." Did Lawson feel chastised and apologize? Far from it. Instead, he doubled down, responding, "Their belief flies in the face of our Constitution. This is not our Bible, we should not be allowing them to pray from that book in our house, just as I do not believe I would be allowed to pray from my Bible in their house." One of the two Muslims who had given the invocation, Naveed Baqir, called Lawson's words "textbook Islamophobia" and invited the bigoted lawmaker to come visit a local mosque to learn about Islam.

Hindu invocations have also occasionally caused a stir. Rajan Zed is a prominent Hindu leader from Reno, Nevada, who has given countless invocations before government bodies all over the United States. When he was scheduled to give the opening prayer at the Idaho Senate in Boise in March 2015, however, three Republican state senators objected and refused to attend. One of them, Steve Vick, from northern Idaho, explained his decision this way: "They have a caste system. They worship cows." One of the others, Sheryl Nuxoll, from Cottonwood, Idaho, proclaimed that "Hindu [sic] is a false faith with false gods" and refused to apologize for the remark. Zed is no stranger to controversy. Many years before the *Town of Greece* decision was handed down, Zed gave an invocation before the U.S. Senate—the first time a Hindu had ever kicked off a session on the Senate floor—and his remarks were interrupted by anti-abortion protestors who screamed at him from the chamber's balcony before being escorted out of the building by Senate police.

As with the case of monuments and displays, secularists have probably been the most active group seeking to join the invocation parade. Americans United launched its Operation Inclusion initiative shortly after the Court's decision in *Town of Greece*, with the goal of ensuring that towns were not discriminating against nonbelievers. As part of this effort, the organization developed legal guidelines for what is and is not allowed under the decision, posted model secular invocations and op-eds for nonbelievers to use, and actively monitored what was going on around the country. The American Humanist Association took similar steps, including creating an interactive map to help Humanists identify individuals in their areas who were willing and able to give nonreligious invocations. The Freedom from Religion Foundation immediately launched Nothing Fails like Prayer, a competition to award $500 prizes to the year's best secular invocations; those prizes have been awarded each year since the *Town of Greece* case was decided and are explicitly intended by the organization to "be a Paine in the government's Mass— a Thomas Paine." Finally, the Central Florida Freethought Community (CFFC, a chapter of FFRF) mobilized to actively bring secular invocations to towns and counties throughout the central Florida region; since 2014, members of the group have given dozens of invocations in some of the most conservative places in the country. The group's website even catalogs the texts of these invocations and provides links to videos of the events if they are available.

Most secular invocations, like those given by minority religions, have occurred without incident. In a telephone conversation I had in 2015 with CFFC leader David Williamson, for example, he told me that he had received no threats and "very little opposition" to the group's efforts. Occasionally, however, the religious majority gets bent out of shape when faced with a secular speech. For instance, in Lake Forest, Florida, in December 2014, four out of five town commissioners, including the mayor, stood up and walked out of the room as soon as Preston Smith, an Atheist, rose to give his invocation. The one commissioner who stayed for the speech, Christopher McVoy, told a reporter that it was "un-American" for the others to walk out and that it was "weird" that they all got up and left at the same time, making him wonder whether the fleeing commissioners had planned the walkout, something that could possibly be illegal under a state law prohibiting commissioners from talking privately about public matters.

In January 2016, when Aleta Ledendecker, a member of a group called Rationalists of East Tennessee, gave a secular invocation at a meeting of the Oak Ridge City Council, one councilwoman skipped the speech, while another got up toward the end and walked out. The member who left, Rick Chinn, explained that he "didn't appreciate what she was saying" and "couldn't take it anymore" because in his opinion "this country was founded on Christian principles." Ledendecker also alleged that the mayor cut her off before she was finished. "I actually found it offensive," she told a local television station. "It was quite rude."

The year 2017 saw a number of disagreements arise over secular invocations. In April, after Democratic Representative Athena Salman gave such an invocation on the floor of the Arizona House of Representatives, Republican lawmakers objected, claiming that the lawmaking body had previously issued guidelines requiring opening invocations to "invoke a higher power." One person even asked for and received permission to give a counter-invocation about Jesus. In the wake of the controversy, the House majority leader, a Christian Republican from Scottsdale named John Allen, announced: "I know it's difficult to understand, but a prayer should be to a higher power. If you don't want to pray, don't sign up for the prayer."

Meanwhile, in Maine, Thomas Waddell, the president of Maine's FFRF chapter, had his invitation to give a secular invocation on the floor of the state Senate rescinded by the Republican Senate president, who asked Waddell to submit the text of his prepared remarks so he could review them before deciding whether to reissue the invitation. And in May in Eustis, Florida, a Christian commissioner insisted on giving a religious invocation after the scheduled secular one by a member of CFFC, noting that the secular group "comes to meetings to antagonize and we won't stand for that."

A couple of places have gone even further in their hostility toward Atheists by trying to outright ban nonbelievers from giving invocations. For instance, in Brevard County, Florida, home to Cocoa Beach and the Kennedy Space Center, the five town commissioners voted unanimously in August 2014 to prohibit Atheists from giving the opening invocation, telling David Williamson in a letter: "The prayer is delivered during the ceremonial portion of the county's meeting, and typically invokes guidance for the County Commission from the highest spiritual authority, a higher authority which a substantial body of Brevard constituents believe to exist." Williamson and some other plaintiffs sued the county, and in September 2017, a federal district court ruled that the government's policy was unconstitutional. In Pennsylvania, the House of Representatives amended its General Operating Rules in late 2014 to stipulate that only a guest who is "a member of a regularly established church or religious organization" may be invited to give the opening prayer. A federal district court found this policy unconstitutional in August 2018, and the case is under appeal as this book goes to press.**

* * *

Linda Stephens lives alone in a modest house less than a five-minute drive from the building where the Town of Greece's town council sits. When I arrived to visit with her, Stephens invited me to take a seat at her dining room table, where we talked at length about her involvement in the big case. Originally from Kalamazoo, Michigan, and still sporting a slight Midwestern accent, Stephens moved to Greece with her husband in the 1970s. When she began attending town meetings in her capacity as a member of a town parks organization, she found the town's practice of beginning each of its sessions with a prayer "irritating," particularly because the prayers were always given by a Christian and usually contained lots of explicit talk about Jesus and other Christian stuff, but initially she would simply grit her teeth and suffer through them. "At first," she told me, "I just bitched about it." When a Jewish resident began demanding the end of the prayer practices, however, Stephens—a former head of the region's AU chapter—was quick to add her voice (and her name) to the effort.

I asked Stephens how her neighbors treated her throughout the years during which her lawsuit had brought so much attention to the otherwise sleepy town. Some people understood, she said, but many did not. Her property was vandalized at least twice. Once someone tore up her mailbox

---

** A similar case involves the U.S. House of Representatives, which denied the request of Dan Barker, co-president of FFRF, to give an Atheist invocation before the House. A district court rejected Barker's challenge to that decision, and FFRF has appealed the judgment to the D.C. Circuit Court of Appeals, which heard arguments in October 2018. The other issue that is currently working its way through the courts is whether members of a town board can offer an opening prayer themselves. From a religious-diversity and non-discrimination perspective, this kind of practice is quite problematic, because it is going to be a rare town board or commission that is made up of, say, a Christian, a Jew, a Buddhist, two Atheists, and a Satanist. Two federal appellate courts have considered this issue and have made different rulings, one holding that the practice is constitutional and the other finding it unconstitutional. It is possible that the Supreme Court will consider the issue at some point to resolve the dispute.

and put it on top of her car; another time, somebody dismantled a fire hydrant and dumped it in her backyard pool. The man who lives behind her told her directly that she should "move out of town" because "nobody likes you." That guy still lives in the same house, but, needless to say, Stephens does not often ask him if she can borrow some sugar.

Stephens would not be the first Atheist to give a secular invocation before the town council in the wake of the Supreme Court's decision. In July 2014, a mere two months after the Court upheld the town's invocation practice, an Atheist from Rochester named Dan Courtney began the council meeting, which was attended by many from the Atheist and Humanist communities, with a roughly three-minute invocation that referenced the framers of the Constitution and Immanuel Kant and asserted that human beings are "the beginning and the end, the alpha and the omega of our destiny." His comments were followed by a round of applause and widely covered in the media. In mid-August, a second Freethinker opened the council meeting, choosing to begin his invocation with an off-color joke. "If you're uncomfortable with an Atheist invocation," he told the five town councillors, "I'll tell you what I tell my wife: it'll be over in three minutes." Stephens cringed as she told me about the joke and the council's reaction, which, unsurprisingly, involved no smiles or laughter. For her turn, Stephens planned something far less idiotic; she was going to use the model Atheist invocation drafted by Americans United, tweaked only slightly for her own purposes.

Although Courtney and the other Atheist had addressed the council since the lawsuit had been decided, neither of them had been intimately involved in the litigation that had made it possible for them to speak there. For this reason, at least to me, Stephens's upcoming invocation was the most symbolically important one yet. Was she excited? It was hard to tell. She seemed a little nervous, which was to be expected. I don't know about you, but I always get nervous when I give an invocation in front of a town council that I just sued for its allegedly unconstitutional invocation practices. I asked Stephens if she expected any controversy at the meeting (the first Atheist invocation attracted only one protestor, a man who stood silently in the corridor outside the meeting room holding a "Jesus Saves" sign). She didn't seem to think there would be a problem, although she also admitted that she didn't know "if the article will stir up anything," a reference to the awkward fact that a reporter had just that day published an article in the *Rochester Democrat and Chronicle* about my trip to watch the invocation.[††] On the question of whether she was glad that she had fought the town's invocation practice generally, however, her answer was emphatic. "I'm very happy that Atheists are giving invocations and coming out of the closet," she told me, with obvious pride in what she was about to do that evening.

* * *

The town of Greece is no Greece, and the town hall of the town of Greece is no Parthenon. The hall lacks historical character, and there's not a Grecian column to be found within a hundred miles of it. Still, though, the place is new and clean and nice enough, and it does have one outstanding feature, which is the brand-new set of blue "pickleball" courts that Bill Reilich, the town supervisor, installed upon taking office. If you've never heard of pickleball, don't worry, I had never heard of it either, even though the website of the USA Pickleball Association claims that about two and a half million Americans participate in the activity. It's sort of like a hybrid of tennis and table tennis, with a weird Wiffle-ball-like sphere that travels at about one-third the speed of a tennis ball. The day I was there nobody was playing on the courts and the fence that enclosed them was locked, so I sadly was not able to investigate this curious sport any further.

I had a four o'clock appointment to meet with Reilich to ask him some questions about the invocation practice and Stephens's planned "prayer," but I arrived at the town hall early, so I wandered through the various displays and bulletin boards on the first floor to see what I could learn about the place. It was pretty typical stuff for a mid-size suburban town—a notice from the Greece Historical Society about a World War II musical

---

[††] As writer David Andreatta put it in that article, "Humorist Visits Greece to See Atheist Invocation": "Most people can't be bothered to travel 400 feet to attend a town board meeting, never mind the 400 miles that Jay Wexler logged to observe a gathering of the Greece board slated for Tuesday."

event, a plaque commemorating soldiers from Greece who died in various wars, a request for bids on a sale of surplus leaf compost, a poster seeking a new family for a dog named Rizzo with "food aggression issues."

At four, I headed upstairs for my appointment, and I was shown into a large office where I sat down to chat with the rotund Reilich and the city's young slick-haired lawyer. Both of them were very friendly and open to answering my questions. We didn't talk for long, but I found out some interesting details, particularly about the procedure the town now uses for scheduling invocations. According to Reilich, once the board establishes the dates for the meetings, it schedules invocations on a first-come, first-served basis. The only limitation is that the group represented by the person giving the invocation must either be from within the town or have a member who is from the town. Reilich explained that the town instituted this policy after people started calling in from all over the country seeking to give an invocation, including someone who wanted to perform an animal sacrifice before a meeting. This was too much for Reilich and the board, even though the sacrificer-in-waiting had offered to bring his own altar.

I tried to get a feel for whether Reilich actually appreciated the opening prayers, but it was hard to tell. He said that the New York State Assembly, where he had previously served, had also started its meeting with a prayer, so the town's practice "did not seem unusual—the same as the Pledge of Allegiance." When I pressed him a little, he said: "There's nothing offensive about them. Does it offer inspiration? A minute or two to pause or privately reflect? There's no harm to that." It seemed to me that with regard to the whole prayer thing he could pretty much take it or leave it, but of course my ability to discern his real feelings on the matter was fairly weak. One thing was for sure, though—he wasn't expecting any conflict or shenanigans over Linda Stephens's invocation. "There won't be any controversy tonight, no," he told me with confidence.

* * *

As it happened, Reilich was right—there wasn't the slightest bit of controversy at all over Stephens's invocation that night. Not even the one guy with the "Jesus Saves" placard showed up. Nobody even said "God" really loudly during the Pledge of Allegiance like I think they did during that first Atheist invocation (I've watched the video of that invocation, but it's not entirely clear). I arrived early and hung out outside the meeting room, trying to look inconspicuous and eavesdrop on nearby conversations to find something juicy to report, but, alas, no luck. The meeting started pretty close to six o'clock, and by the time it got under way, the room was packed with people, including a lot of police officers in full uniform. They were attending to be promoted rather than to protect Stephens from angry rioters. I sat in the back corner with my little notebook, in case anything interesting happened. Reilich called the meeting to order, and after the Pledge of Allegiance and a brief discussion of the new police station building that is in the works, he invited Stephens to "lead us in a moment of prayer."

Dressed conservatively in black pants and a gray cardigan over a white shirt, Stephens stood and addressed the town councillors from a podium that had been turned toward the bench at an angle (the Supreme Court decision had emphasized that the invocations were more for the council members than the audience). She started off a little shaky but gained strength as the invocation went on. This is what she said:

> Good evening. I would like to thank Supervisor Reilich and the Town Board members for allowing me to deliver the invocation this evening. I am a member of Sunday Assembly Rochester, which is a secular congregation popularly known as an "atheist church." Sunday Assembly welcomes non-theists of all stripes including atheists, agnostics, humanists, free-thinkers and other like-minded people. On a personal note, I am sometimes disappointed with the quality of the invocations given before the town board meetings, including the atheist ones. For that reason, I sought help with this one tonight. I hope you find it acceptable.

> The Town of Greece is a big town. Nearly 100,000 people live here, many different kinds of people. Sometimes this can present problems, but more often than not, it's a source of our strength. Greece residents do not all think the same way or believe the same things. Yet, it is important to remember that we are all linked by our common humanity and our shared origin. When we work together to move our town forward in a spirit of

mutual respect and common decency, we showcase what is best about our community, our state, and our nation.

The residents of Greece have diverse beliefs. We are Christians, Jews, Muslims, Hindus, Buddhists, humanists, atheists, agnostics, Wiccans, Pagans, Sikhs, and that's not all. We are straight, gay, and transgender. We are young and old and everything in between. We are of different races and nationalities. Some of us are liberal; some of us are conservative; and some of us are a bit of both. It is not surprising then that we do not agree about everything. And we often feel fiercely protective of what we do believe. There is great passion in our beliefs—and rightly so.

But there is one thing on which we can all agree. We share the goal of making our community the best place it can be. We unite here this evening around that noble aim and common purpose. Thank you.

I am genuinely happy to report that during the invocation, I heard no boos, no groans, no hisses, nothing. As far as I could tell, the crowd of about eighty people remained quiet and respectful throughout the entire speech. The man sitting next to me did take his baseball hat off when Supervisor Reilich announced that someone was going to lead a "prayer," and then about thirty seconds later put the hat back on when he realized that nobody was really giving a prayer, but other than that the entire episode was completely uneventful.‡‡

It turned out that most of the people in the audience were there to see the police officers be sworn in to their new positions. Families watched and smiled with pride as these six men and women put their hands on the Bible and swore to God that they would carry out their duties with honor. After that, probably half the audience left. I was determined to stay to the end, however, so I settled in for the "public forum" section of the evening, during which someone spoke out passionately against the installation of a pavilion at some lake beach and someone else spoke really loudly about the environmental hazards threatening the town's creeks. After that, a restaurant that "pairs high quality meats with wines and wine flights" made its

---

‡‡ It was a Red Sox hat, incidentally. #YankeesSuck.

case to be granted a special-use permit for operation at a city plaza. Finally, with only maybe a dozen other people left in the room (Linda Stephens was one of them), I listened to the town board go one by one without any discussion through twenty-nine agenda items. You'll be happy to know, I'm sure, that the town supervisor was granted authorization to purchase and implement a new payroll software system. About an hour after the meeting began, it was adjourned. I said my good-byes to Stephens in the town hall parking lot and zipped off to the liquor store before it closed to buy two tiny bottles of Jameson for my own little private celebration in my motel room near the airport.

The next day, Stephens sent me a link to a letter to the editor that had appeared in the morning's newspaper, titled "Why Do Atheists Expend the Energy?" A certain Gregg Miesch from Hilton, New York, was confused about why an Atheist would "get bent out of shape about someone, (God), who they say doesn't even exist." He continued:

> Do they also spend time, money, energy, and frustration trying to convince people that Santa and the Easter bunny don't exist? Here's (one) of their problems: if you ask an atheist what the purpose of life is, they'll likely tell you, at least in part, "To be happy." Why then, go to such lengths to dissuade those of us who are happy, even joyful, believing in God? If there's no God, no eternal consequence for the life lived, there is no meaningful purpose, and all is futile. All efforts to be happy amount to nothing—no remembrance of happiness, no future, no hope. It all ends up to zero.

Sheesh—he says this like it's a bad thing!§§

* * *

Gregg Miesch's brilliant commentary to the side, I think that secular legislative invocations like the one Linda Stephens delivered in Greece

---

§§ A number of people posted comments in response, like John Dale, who wrote: "If [you] try to get people to live by a set of archaic and bigoted rules as dictated by the Easter Bunny, then I guarantee that there will be hordes of Easter Bunny non-believers opposing you."

are extremely important, because they can help educate both the general population and individuals serving in government about the content and teachings of Humanism and other secular belief systems. Of course, what goes for Atheism goes too for other minority groups, including minority faiths like Wicca, Hinduism, and the like. The invocation, if done well, can resemble a two- or three-minute mini lecture on the faith, given in front of a captive audience that will necessarily include (unless they leave to avoid the invocation) some of the most powerful and influential members of the community. This is part of what Linda Stephens was referring to when she told me she was happy that Atheists were coming out of the closet. As she told prominent Atheist Heman Mehta in an interview:

> This Supreme Court case has proved to be a very good thing for atheists. It's clear now that *Town of Greece v Galloway* is one of those "We lost the battle, but we won the war" situations. Before the Court's ruling last May, it was highly unusual for an atheist to be allowed to deliver an invocation at a government meeting. After the ruling, atheists and other secularists all over the country have begun delivering invocations, even in places like the deep South. I am pleased with what has happened and hope more and more non-theists will avail themselves of this opportunity. It's a wonderful way to make the public realize that we are equal citizens.

Others have made similar points. For instance, in response to an e-mail to Rajan Zed in which I asked him why he thought it was important for Hindus to give invocations, he responded: "To create dialogue, as dialogue brings us mutual enrichment and assists us in vanquishing stereotypes and prejudices passed on to us from previous generations. To highlight that we have more in common than in conflict." Of all the people I spoke to about the issue, though, David Williamson might have put it the best, when he told me:

> Regardless of whether I or anyone else thinks these prayers should stop and regardless of the victory that might be, I challenge anyone to tell me of a better time and place to get the message out about the secular values of inclusion, diversity, tolerance, and equality to the folks that need to

hear it the most. When I or anyone else is doing an invocation, everyone at the meeting is standing at attention and is primed to conduct the business of the day. I am having a hard time coming to the conclusion that these invocations should stop. It is valuable activism to undertake and a venue which we never took advantage of before.

All I can say to that is: *Amen.*

* * *

As I hope I've demonstrated in these first few chapters, Christian majorities often do not react well when Atheists and minority religious groups demand their rightful place in American public life. But if you want to see these people *really* freak out, you have to watch what happens when the Satanists show up. Chapter 4 will tackle that topic.

4

THE SATANIC TEMPLE

Taking It to a Whole 'Nother Level

THE TOWN OF BELLE PLAINE is so small that it makes the town of Greece look like Athens in comparison, or at least Thessaloniki. I did make it to Belle Plaine in July 2017, but not under the circumstances I had expected. On the night before Saturday morning's planned rally against the Satanic veterans monument, I received an e-mail message from TST's Doug Mesner informing me that the town council would be deciding at its Monday meeting whether to revoke the limited public forum it had created back in February. Predicting another heated and exciting meeting like the one that had taken place earlier in the year, I immediately booked a flight to Minneapolis for Sunday morning. By noon on Sunday I had checked into my room at the HomeTown Inn and Suites, which is close enough to Veterans Memorial Park that you can see it from the parking lot.

It's a shame that I wasn't able to make it to the Saturday rally because by all accounts it was quite an event. About 150 Catholics, most from out of town (and one holding a statue of the Virgin Mary on his shoulders), showed up at the park to protest, praying and holding signs saying things like "Honk against Satan," "Keep It One Nation under God," and "Satan Is the Eternal Loser." Nearby, a group from the Minnesota Left Hand Path Community supported the monument while lounging on some picnic blankets, where they ate snacks and talked with both protestors and the media. According to the Left Hand folks, they made at least one convert during the protest, and it "wasn't even because of the cookies and lemonade."

The day I arrived, I drove out to a Starbucks in nearby Shakopee to chat with Koren Walsh and Kimber Starnes, two members of the Left Hand Path, about their experiences with TST, the monument, and the rally. Walsh and Starnes told me that there are about twenty or twenty-five people in their Left Hand Path Community ("Left Hand," they explained, refers to people who look inside the self for meaning, like Atheists, Satanists, and Buddhists—people who, as Starnes put it, "are working out spiritual shit on their own"). They had helped run a chapter of TST for a while, but the chapter left the national organization over differences in opinion about some of TST's decisions. Because TST's monument was going to be placed basically in their backyard, though, Walsh, Starnes, and some other likeminded people raised $1,000 for the black cube by selling cupcakes made by Walsh, with penises and vaginas on them, and "coffin cookies" designed by Starnes, an accomplished artist whose work focuses primarily on death. "As much as I don't want religion, I really want this statue," Walsh told me. "We made so many cupcakes."

I asked Walsh and Starnes about the rally the day before, and they both told me it had been fairly incredible. Walsh said she barely had time to eat because she spent most of the rally talking to reporters. I had seen some of the interviews she gave online; in one of them she told a reporter that she was frightened of the protestors, primarily because she had received "threats of rape, of murder, or both." I asked about this, and both Walsh and Starnes admitted to being shaken by the presence of so many people at the park. Starnes was particularly traumatized. "I felt terrified," the death artist told me, "and it takes a lot to terrify me." Her fear and disease were clearly exacerbated by the current state of the nation. Calling Donald Trump the "Fascist Cheeto," Starnes told me, "I don't want to be on this planet anymore. Things sucked before, but it wasn't this bad." A few minutes later, however, she said that she had found a real home among the Left Hand Path Community in Minneapolis and now feels like "it's all right to exist in the world exactly as I am."

I spent most of Monday in my hotel room, working and waiting for the evening meeting of the town board, but a brief afternoon stroll over to Veterans Memorial Park brought an interesting surprise. I was sitting on a bench under a tree, admiring how the park's prairie grasses and American flags move lightly in the wind together, when I noticed out of the corner of my eye a woman walking around the circumference of the park holding a large jug of water. At first I thought she might have been exercising and drinking from the jug to stay hydrated, but then I realized that every couple of yards, she would stop and sprinkle a little water from the jug onto the ground. She was blessing the park with holy water! I had never seen such a thing, so I sat and watched as unobtrusively as possible, as the woman wandered over to the public forum part of the park, right where the Joe monument had been (Joe had been removed before the rallies, purportedly to protect it in case things got out of hand). The woman poured the remaining water from the jug directly on that spot. She then stood for about two minutes holding a cross up in both hands in front of her, presumably praying. When she was done, she looked over at me and waved. I waved back, and she left.

I'm sad to report that the town board meeting on Monday evening was one of the most anticlimactic two-hour periods of my life. The resolution rescinding the public forum was shoved into the middle of a long list of agenda items that were approved at the beginning of the meeting by consent, without any public debate or discussion. Just like that, with the snap of a finger, the public forum was gone. Although I sat there for the rest of the meeting, along with about forty other people, just in case anything about the forum came up, nothing interesting happened; most of the meeting was spent in a heated debate over whether the board should grant a motion for a zoning variance to allow an apartment building to go up on the corner of Church and Alpine Streets (the motion failed).

It turned out that all the discussion and debate about the public forum had taken place either by e-mail or in private. TST had obtained a stack of e-mail messages about the issue that residents of Belle Plaine and nearby towns had sent to the city manager. Although there were one or two that supported the inclusion of the Satanic monument, the rest were opposed, often hysterically so, to the notion. For example:

> All good Christians know it is true that when Jesus knocks on your door and you let Him in He will bring into your house good gifts. . . . It is also true that when Satan knocks at your door, and you let him in he will bring bad gifts. Gifts like immorality, impurity, sensuality, idolatry, sorcery, enmities, strife, jealousy, outbursts of anger, disputes, dissensions, factions, envying, drunkenness, and death. . . . Please do not invite Satan in to your beautiful city. Please reject the Satanist monument in memorial park.

> Even the thought of a monument to Satan is shocking. The horror of honoring Satan, the father of lies, the evil one, the enemy of mankind is truly beyond my ability to articulate. Please do not bend to some aberrant minority to appease them. . . . Setting aside the spiritual question, who would ever want to go visit Belle Plaine if it is a place that invites in evil and darkness?

> Are you nuts or just plane [sic] dumb, why would anyone want to subject their community to this kind of notoriety?

> I'm writing you about this disgraceful satanic monument your [sic] putting up next to the veterans, are you people that depraved, you put up evil near something so sacred, as long as you have this atrocity, I'll NEVER come to your city as long as you have this. You people are sick, and so morbid.

> Are you ready to deal with, and have on your conscience, tortured and mutilated cats? This isn't just a Halloween thing, nor just black cats, it's constant. Do you want your or your neighbors' cats stolen? Do you want your animal shelter to be providing cats for torture or is the mission of your shelter to try and find GOOD homes for the cats? Do you want your families and children to find the remains over and over and over again? This nuisance alone—hoping it's against your city law to torture and kill cats—should be grounds enough to deny the viability of a satanic memorial/altar in your city. . . . Sad.

Somewhat deflated by the meeting, I walked a block down the town's main street to Johan's Sports Bar and Grill for a burger and some beers. Bingo had just ended, and so after a group of older people filed out, the bar was almost empty. I asked the bartender what he thought about the whole Satanic monument controversy, and he declared that he was happy that his town had stood up to the Satanists. A young couple sat down near me, and we all talked some more about the situation while I stuffed my face with delicious tater tots. The woman also seemed happy about the result and was excited to explain that "if someone believes in Satan, they must also believe in God," a sentiment that the bartender enthusiastically affirmed. A second bartender, though, seemed a little more thoughtful about the whole thing; she expressed her disappointment that the Catholics who had come from out of town to protest the Satanic monument were more concerned about religion than they were about veterans. The guy from the young couple echoed the focus on veterans; he said he didn't really have an opinion on religion but felt strongly that veterans should be honored. An older guy came in later who actually seemed to have some sympathy for TST's position, but the only thing he said that I can remember for certain was in response to the young lady's confession that although Catholic, she did not believe in hell. "Well, then," he replied, "you've never been to Idaho."

After a few beers, I made my way back to the Home View Inn and Suites for the night and then back to Boston the next morning. The last I heard, Joe had been put on display above the entrance to the private Belle Plaine Vets Club. The Satanic Temple moved the veterans monument to its headquarters in Salem, Massachusetts, and filed suit against Belle Plaine to try and get back the money it spent having the monument constructed.

* * *

Back in 2015, when I first embarked on writing this book, TST was one group among many that was working on bringing alternative religious views to the public square. As I continued researching and writing, however, it became clear that TST has risen to the forefront of the movement that I was trying to describe and evaluate. Because the group is so central to my story, and because Satanism tends to be wildly misunderstood by most people, I decided that it would make sense to devote an entire chapter to TST and its efforts.

To understand TST, it is important to know at least something about the history of Satanism in the United States and elsewhere.* Let's start with a question: What comes to mind when you think of Satanism? Child sacrifice? Blood drinking? Black magic? Grave desecration? Certainly the torture and mutilation of cats! If your answer included one or more of these things, you surely have lots of company. But here's what you should do with those answers: put them in a trash bag, take the trash bag to the dump, and set it on fire. The idea that Satanists are child-sacrificing evildoers comes entirely from the media and from movies and from those who were responsible for manufacturing and spreading the now completely debunked "Satanic Panic" of the 1980s and 1990s. In other words, what you have heard about Satanism probably comes from what people who are not Satanists say about Satanists, and not from Satanists themselves.

This distinction between what scholars of modern Satanism (and there is a lot of recent scholarship on the topic—Oxford University Press, in fact, published several substantial volumes on Satanism between 2013 and 2016 alone) call "attribution" and "identification" is extremely important when talking about any kind of religion. Consider Judaism, for example. A lot of people out there think that the Jews are orchestrating an international banking conspiracy to rule the world, but no reasonable person would conclude that therefore taking over the world's banking system is an actual tenet of Judaism. Why should we approach Satanism any differently? When it comes to understanding Satanism, it is particularly crucial to listen to what the people who actually *identify* as Satanists say about what they believe and what they do.

What is Satanism, anyway? Those who study the topic have developed a variety of definitions. One scholar has proposed this as a definition:

---

* What follows is a very simplified account of the history of Satanism. The notes at the end of the book contain citations to numerous sources for those who wish to pursue the matter further.

"Satanism is a *system* where Satan is the only or the foremost of the divinities, personages, or principles being venerated." Another has suggested that a Satanist is an "individual in whose worldview or belief system Satan—regardless of Satan being conceived as personal entity, impersonal force, or symbol—is revered as the crucial, fundamental, and/or ultimate principle." Using definitions like these, scholars have basically concluded that before the eighteenth century, there were very few instances of actual Satanism to be found. Some people here and there venerated Satan in some way, and an extremely limited Satanic subculture in France may have existed in the late-seventeenth and early-eighteenth centuries, but no groups before the modern age systematically worshipped the devil. Of course, *attribution* of devil worship was widespread. Christians have "demonized" others, including Jews, "witches," and other heretics as Satanists since at least the Middle Ages, but as I just explained, this has nothing to do with the history of genuine Satanism.

Perhaps surprisingly, the basis for much of modern Satanism comes from literature, most notably John Milton's publication of *Paradise Lost* in 1667 and the "Romantic Satanists" of the late eighteenth century who followed him. These writers were not Satanists in the sense of the definitions recited above—poets like William Blake and Percy Bysshe Shelley and Lord Byron did not venerate the devil—but they did recast the character of Satan as a positive figure embodying Enlightenment values such as individual freedom, rational and critical thought, scientific knowledge, sexual liberation, and social reform. These writers found it useful to reinvent traditional Christian symbols as a way of expressing their rejection of traditional authority and dogmatism. As one scholar puts it: "In an inversion of traditional (and more conventional contemporary) usages of Satan as the moving power behind the enemy, he became a symbol for the struggle against tyranny, injustice, and oppression. He was made into a mythical figure of rebellion for an age of revolutions, a larger-than-life individual for an age of individualism, a free thinker in an age struggling for free thought."

Although scholars have identified a few isolated instances of true Satanism in the interim between the Romantics and the 1960s (some, for example, have referred to Polish writer Stanislaw Przybyszewski [1868–1927] as the "first

Satanist"), it was not until Anton LaVey founded the Church of Satan in 1966 in San Francisco that a systematic, developed, and popular Satanism came into being. The key "scripture" of the Church is LaVey's *The Satanic Bible*, which he published in 1969 and which has sold more than a million copies since.

LaVey and his Satanism are hard to characterize, but a few things are clear. Like the Romantic Satanists of earlier centuries, LaVey did not believe in Satan as an actual supernatural figure, but rather venerated Satan as a symbol of rebellion, free thought, and sexuality. His form of Satanism was also deeply colored by an Ayn Rand–esque social Darwinism; indeed, the first part of *The Satanic Bible* was largely adapted from an earlier text titled *Might Is Right*, written by a pseudonymous author named Ragnar Redbeard. In its early years, the highly organized and hierarchical church was centered in San Francisco, where LaVey held regular Satanic rituals and workshops in his home. By the early 1970s, however, he ceased public activities in San Francisco, and for a few years the church revolved around local chapters throughout the country known as "grottos." In 1975, LaVey disbanded the grottos, and around the same time a large and prominent contingent of the church, including High Priest Michael Aquino, left to form the Temple of Set, a splinter group that worships the Egyptian god Set (who the Temple believes is the first and true Prince of Darkness) as a literal being.

These developments, of course, somewhat undermined the vitality of the church, but it still exists today. LaVey died in 1997, and the church is now run from New York City (Hell's Kitchen, to be exact) by his successor, a high priest named Peter Gilmore. The church maintains a website that contains a wealth of information about its history and tenets, including this passage from the site's front page:

> We are the first above-ground organization in history openly dedicated to the acceptance of Man's true nature—that of a carnal beast, living in a cosmos that is indifferent to our existence. To us, Satan is the symbol that best suits the nature of we who are carnal by birth—people who feel no battles raging between our thoughts and feelings, we who do not embrace the concept of a soul imprisoned in a body. He represents pride, liberty, and individualism—qualities often defined as Evil by those who worship external deities, who feel there is a war between their minds and emotions.

Between the mid-1970s and the mid-1990s, true Satanism fell into disarray. As one scholar puts it, "[M]odern Satanism became a splintered and disorganized movement. . . . Satanism seemed to exist in such relative obscurity that [yet another scholar] almost declared it extinct." It was during this period that fundamentalist Christians, aided by discredited psychotherapists touting "recovered memory therapy" and a media seeking sensationalist headlines, began widely and falsely accusing so-called Satanists of various types of ritual abuse and murder in what is now referred to as the "Satanism Scare" or the "Satanic Panic." Many of these accusations focused on day care centers, where claims were made of

> [t]he appearance of strange men and women with only one arm, some limping and some with tattooed bodies; Devil worship; secret subterranean tunnels; burned or cooked and eaten babies; murdered and mutilated babies; ceremonies and other activities held in basements; physical abuse . . . mock marriages; nude photography; molesters of different races; Christmas-tree lights; children handcuffed or tied with rope; various objects ranging from screwdrivers to crayons inserted in rectums and vaginas; drowned people or animals; clandestine visits to cemeteries . . . oral sex on virtually anyone and even on animals; drug-taking; blood drunk or used in ceremonies; pornographic films; burial of children; urination and defecation . . . and so on.

Happily, according to a scholar of the time period, much of this panic over Satanism quickly dissipated, as "critical academics, lawyers, ex-patients, journalists, and police officers dismantled the claims." "By the mid-1990s," the scholar continues, "professional and public opinion had shifted, and SRA [Satanic ritual abuse] was recognized as a moral panic of the kind that had driven earlier witch-hunts."

The next main chapter of real Satanism began in the mid-1990s with the growing availability of the Internet, which allowed like-minded people to connect and share information with one another. In the past twenty years, a number of small Satanic groups have formed, mostly aided by the Web. These groups share the veneration of Satan in some form, but beyond that characteristic it is difficult to generalize about them. Some believe that Satan is a real being, but many, if not most, are atheistic, following the

Romantics and LaVey in treating Satan as a powerful symbol rather than as a literal entity. Some groups emphasize certain Satanic themes—sexuality, freedom, science—more than others do. Some, like the group known as the Order of Nine Angles, are part of what has been termed "the Sinister Tradition," meaning, among other things, that its members "despise any kind of ethical behavior"; most groups, however, do not subscribe to that tradition. It is impossible to know how many people worldwide believe in Satan, but one estimate from 2009 put the number of true Satanists at somewhere between 30,000 and 100,000.

* * *

The Satanic Temple was founded in 2012 and moved from scattered physical and online locations to its national headquarters in Salem in the fall of 2016. The organization is currently run by a national council, which oversees a collection of local chapters around the country and abroad. The number of chapters has varied over time as some are added and others leave the fold, but as I'm writing this, the Temple's website lists sixteen. Some of the more active chapters include those in New York, Arizona, and Seattle, the last of which is run by Lilith Starr, a Harvard and Stanford graduate whose "About the Author" information for her 2015 book, *The Happy Satanist*, notes that she lives with her "husband and full-time slave, Uruk Black." Now, here's a little quiz:

> If we want to understand what TST believes and is all about, we should start by listening to the views of . . .
>
> A) The citizens of Belle Plaine, Minnesota.
>
> B) The Church of Satan, which thinks TST is "a marketing stunt, turned activist group, using purposefully inflammatory imagery and silly stunts to gain media attention and promote their sociopolitical agendas."
>
> C) Tucker Carlson, who, in an interview with Doug Mesner on Fox TV, barked: "The point of calling this 'Satanism' is to horrify, like, normal people in the middle of the country."

D) Jason Rapert, theocratic Senator from Arkansas, who has claimed that TST is "mentally ill."

E) The Satanic Temple.

Did you answer "E"? If so, then yay, you! Luckily, the organization has put a good deal of information about itself on its website. Obviously you can look at the site yourself to learn more, but a few points are worth repeating here. The first thing to note is that like the Romantics and the Church of Satan, TST does not conceive of Satan as a personal being but rather as a symbol. Specifically, the website states: "Satan is symbolic of the Eternal Rebel in opposition to arbitrary authority, forever defending personal sovereignty even in the face of insurmountable odds. Satan is an icon for the unbowed will of the unsilenced inquirer . . . the heretic who questions sacred laws and rejects all tyrannical impositions. Ours is the literary Satan best exemplified by Milton and the Romantic Satanists, from Blake to Shelley, to Anatole France." Second, the site makes it clear how TST differs from the Church of Satan. There are several distinctions, but probably the most important one is that TST "reject[s] LaVeyan social Darwinist rhetoric that fails to agree with what is currently known regarding social evolution." In other words, while TST maintains the emphasis on individual will that characterized LaVeyan Satanism, it has jettisoned the obnoxious "Might Is Right"/Ayn Rand theme that characterized the Church of Satan. Finally, the website lists the group's "Seven Tenets," which are the cornerstone of TST's philosophical and religious beliefs:

- One should strive to act with compassion and empathy towards all creatures in accordance with reason.

- The struggle for justice is an ongoing and necessary pursuit that should prevail over laws and institutions.

- One's body is inviolable, subject to one's own will alone.

- The freedoms of others should be respected, including the freedom to offend. To willfully and unjustly encroach upon the freedoms of another is to forgo one's own.

- Beliefs should conform to our best scientific understanding of the world. We should take care never to distort scientific facts to fit our beliefs.

- People are fallible. If we make a mistake, we should do our best to rectify it and remediate any harm that may have been caused.

- Every tenet is a guiding principle designed to inspire nobility in action and thought. The spirit of compassion, wisdom, and justice should always prevail over the written or spoken word.

The Satanic Temple takes these tenets seriously. They are repeated often in the group's public information and materials, and members tend to mention them in conversations with the media and others. When I was in Salt Lake City investigating the Summum, I happened upon a public meeting held by TST's Utah chapter (which no longer exists) at the beautiful Salt Lake public library in a fourth-floor room that looks out at the original statehouse.[†] About fifty curious men and women—mostly on the young side, almost all wearing black (my friend Adrienne, eternal rebel that she is, showed up wearing the brightest neon yellow shirt I've ever seen), many sporting hairdos and makeup that undoubtedly would have impressed the members of KISS—gathered to hear Chapter Head Chalice Blythe describe the beliefs and mission of TST while they munched on chips and other snacks provided by the Temple. Blythe, whose looks and manner seemed to Adrienne and me like a mashup of Sarah Vowell and Janeane Garofalo, spent a lot of time explaining the tenets to the group, putting them in somewhat more colloquial language. Commenting on the first tenet, for instance, Blythe described it as basically, "Don't be a dick—nobody likes a dick." Tenet number three, for its part, was paraphrased as "I can't punch this guy in the face." On the individual-freedom point, a skeptical woman with a green ponytail asked Blythe whether TST would tell her what to say or do, and Blythe answered with a decisive "No," although another TST guy named Paul followed this up with, "You have to eat our fucking snacks."

---

†   For those counting at home, that's two quirky religious groups I investigated in Salt Lake City, neither of which was the Mormons.

If the list of TST tenets reminds you of the platform of a radical leftist political organization, you have probably understood them correctly. TST is a highly politically active group, taking positions so far to the left that they make Bernie Sanders look like Joe Lieberman. I'll have plenty to say about the group's church-state activities in a minute, but first I should mention a number of other TST activist campaigns that do not get nearly the same amount of media attention, including its "Grey Faction" work, aimed at righting the continuing wrongs of the Satanic Panic era; its "Protect Children Project," which campaigns against corporal punishment in schools; and its "Religious Reproductive Rights" campaign, which has sued Missouri over the state's requirement that women wait seventy-two hours before getting an abortion (TST claims that the requirement is unconstitutional as it applies to TST members who believe in the inviolability of one's body). The Temple is also incredibly inviting and supportive of the LGBTQ community. As *Vice* magazine's Kate Ryan, who "identifies as both gay and queer—queer in the modern sense of rejecting binary thinking," writes: "[T]he Temple is an important movement that provides a safe, radically-inclusive space for people who identify in all sorts of ways. Without defining itself as an LGBTQ organization outright, the Satanic Temple has become a haven for queer folks. At the first meeting I attended, nearly everyone I talked to was confidently queer, gay, pansexual, transgender, bi, polyamorous, or something in between."

With all the media hoopla about TST's church-state activities, it is easy to overlook not only these other policy-based campaigns, but also all of the religious activities that TST sponsors primarily for its members and allies. Without understanding the full range of TST's offerings, though, one can fall into the trap of mistakenly thinking that the group is simply a parody organization whose only goal is to expose blatant violations of church-state separation. Like devotees of most other religions, TST members participate in rituals both at the headquarters in Salem (for example, a Black Mass on Halloween 2017 and Walpurgisnacht at the end of April in 2016) and around the country (including a Satanic Cleansing in Arizona, an Unbaptism ritual in Salt Lake City, and a Satanic Mass in Los Angeles). TST has ordained officiants who can conduct services, including weddings, and it sponsors lectures on a wide range of theological, historical, and ethical issues of interest to the community, with titles like "Queer Satanism," "Ritualized Resistance," "Why Satan? Understanding Modern Satanism," and "Witches, Sluts, Feminists: Unleashing the Demon Feminine," to name just a few. Art and symbolism are particularly important to the Temple, and indeed in the TST headquarters building, which houses the Salem Art Gallery, the group sponsors exhibitions by artists who work in the Satanic tradition, like Chris Andres (the designer of the monument to veterans), Mark Porter, and Vincent Castiglia (who paints in human blood). I've been to the headquarters on several occasions, and I can attest to the awesomeness of some of this art, although I would definitely counsel that it is not for everybody.

* * *

Although TST engages in many different activities, it is undoubtedly true that most non-Satanists who have heard of the Temple know about it because of its church-state related campaigns. More than any other group, TST has actively and vociferously demanded that if Christians can take part in public life, others (even Satanists!) should be able to do so on the exact same terms.

Satanists have ruffled feathers all across the country by asking to give invocations at local governmental meetings. Some of these events have gone relatively smoothly, all things considered. For instance, although a group of Christians protested a 2017 Satanic invocation outside the Grand Junction, Colorado, City Hall, the event was mostly without incident. A Satanist named Andrew Vodopich, who is himself not actually a member of TST, spoke for about a minute, beseeching "all those present to shun primitive hatreds and superstition, bigotry, prejudice and atavism and instead seek equality in justice and thereby safeguard all worldviews and treat them equally and with respect"; he then concluded with the two words that all Satanists like to hear: "Hail Satan." Reactions were muted, even supportive. One resident, who came to the meeting just to see how it would go, told a newspaper that he might want to try giving a pro-cannabis invocation sometime, adding: "I wouldn't mind seeing a Rastafarian up there."

Other events have not gone so smoothly. In Pensacola, Florida, the July 2016 city council meeting at which TST member David Suhor was scheduled to give an invocation turned out to be anything but orderly. As Suhor—dressed in a long black robe with a hood over his head—approached the podium to begin his remarks, Christians who filled the chamber stood and began delivering the Lord's Prayer to drown him out. Charles Bare, the president of the council, tried to get the crowd to settle down by asking them if they would "at least keep it . . . low," but even this polite request was rejected. One protestor yelled, "No! He's going to bring curses on us and you." Eventually, after Bare asked the police to clear the room of anyone who was unwilling to keep quiet, Suhor was able to give his invocation, a loud and deep chanting of phrases like "Let us embrace the Luciferian impulse to eat of the tree of knowledge" and "Let us demand that individuals be judged for their concrete actions, not their fealty to arbitrary social norms and illusory categorizations." The inevitable "Hail Satan" was delivered in a booming crescendo that may have awakened several of the town's light nappers.

On the Kenai Peninsula, which extends southwest from Anchorage, Alaska, a TST invocation in August 2016 resulted in months of frenzied legislative and judicial activity. Iris Fontana, a twenty-seven-year-old college student who explained, "Satan is a symbol . . . and we really just want to embody speaking out against things that are kind of indoctrinated into our culture," gave an invocation before the Kenai Borough Assembly that was similar to Suhor's, at least in its language if not its tone. Only one of the assembly members actually left the area during the invocation, immediately returning after it was over, so there was no actual disruption of the invocation. Afterward, however, following at least one public Christian protest, the assembly adopted a new invocation policy limiting who can give the opening invocation to members of religious associations that are established in and regularly meet within the borough. The ACLU spent months trying to persuade the assembly that such a restriction is unconstitutional, but finally in late 2016, after not meeting any success, the group sued the borough. In October 2018, a superior court in Alaska ruled that the borough's policy violated the state's constitution.

Nowhere has a proposed TST invocation been more controversial, however, than in Phoenix, Arizona. In December 2015, a couple of TST members named Michelle Shortt and Stu De Haan asked the city council if they could deliver an invocation before the legislative body, and the council agreed, scheduling them to give the opening invocation at the body's February 17, 2016, meeting. When this became widely known in the Phoenix community, however, a lot of people predictably went bananas. The city council, responding to public pressure to exclude the Satanists, met on February 3 to consider a motion by one of its members to replace the city's invocation practice with a moment of silence. During the meeting, which was attended by more than a hundred people and lasted several hours, members of the community approached a podium at the front of the room and spoke for two minutes each about their opinions on the motion.

I watched footage of the entire meeting and found it excruciating. Although a few tolerant folks spoke in favor either of letting the Satanists give their invocation or of shutting down the prayer practice entirely and replacing it with the moment of silence, the vast majority of people who spoke urged the council to simply ban the Satanists from speaking. Their comments were filled with hate and ignorance; not a single speaker was familiar with the tenets or beliefs of TST, and almost no one showed any appreciation for religious diversity or respect for the beliefs of others. When you read the selection of comments that I've reproduced below—most of which were met with raucous applause—remember that these speakers were not worshipping in a *church*, but rather were expressing their opinions in a *public forum* on whether two people who disagree with the majority religious viewpoint should be allowed to speak for about two minutes before a *governmental body* that is supposed to serve every resident of Phoenix:

- "We take a Pledge of Allegiance. It's one nation under God. That's not there by mistake."

- [Man taking out a dollar bill:] "I do believe it says 'in God we trust.' I will stand for God every single time. Satanists are a cult. We're gonna pray to God, and that's what we're gonna do."

- "A moment of silence [would be] a total disrespect for our Creator. . . . Don't sell your souls on this."

- "This nation has been a holy nation. . . . We continue to honor the Creator of our nation and our world because if we abandon Him, He will abandon us."

- "What you bring into our city, you will answer to God. We exalt Jesus Christ."

- [A person nearly breaking down in tears:] "I'm a Christian. I believe in the one true God. I want Christians to pray. We need healing in our land. We don't need another curse on our land. It breaks my heart to hear what's going on. I believe in God."

- "Satanists will bring curses."

- "Lift up in the name of Jesus! Make no mistake about it, Jesus is the way!"

- "This is evil against good and the devil is out to win and we don't want to give him Phoenix. When Satan is in control he comes to steal, kill, and destroy, we don't want that for Phoenix. It's either God or it's Satan, good or evil, it has to be one or the other."

- "The nation that forgets God shall be turned into hell. I'd like to ask you all today not to forget God in what you're doing. You have the power to not let our city Phoenix Arizona our state to be turned into hell."

- "Do not open the door to one who steals and destroys."

- "Our goal is to shut down [the Satanists' agenda], which is to bring death and destruction over Phoenix."

- "Don't mock God. When you do so you will reap what you sow. Do not invoke a cult."

- "I'm a child of God. Do we want God in this room, or don't we? So we as a city can be blessed."

- "I can't imagine having a Satanist church come here and invoke the powers of darkness over the people of Phoenix, when most people pray every day to keep him away from us."

The most distasteful comments of the evening were spouted by a young-ish woman with dyed red hair named Monica Dennington, a minister at something called Tic Toc Ministries. Dennington, who clearly had no genuine knowledge about TST whatsoever, nonetheless accused the Temple of being a "misogynist" "hate group" that "is against the God of nature" and "promotes violence against women" and vilified its spokesperson as a terrorist who utters "slurs against gays and Jews." Dennington's testimony was made even worse by the fact that the city council allowed her to speak far longer than the allotted two minutes and was explicitly supported by Councilman Sal DiCiccio, who referred to TST during their exchange as a "cult, not a real religion." DiCiccio went on to accuse TST of having the "main goal . . . to silence the other side," which is fairly amazing given that the whole point of the three-hour meeting was to figure out how to silence the Satanists.

In the end, the city council decided to avoid both lawsuits and the Satanist invocation by voting to end its invocation practice and instituting a moment of silence instead.‡ The council, in other words, had chosen silence over religious diversity. "It was," DiCiccio tweeted after the meeting, "a sad day for Phoenix."

* * *

The Belle Plaine Veterans Monument controversy was hardly the first time that TST has raised hackles by attempting to install a Satanic display in public. A couple of times, the Temple has actually succeeded in placing its imagery on government property. During the holiday season in 2016, for instance, a local schoolteacher and TST member erected a ten-foot-tall, three-hundred-pound red pentagram next to a Nativity scene in a park in Boca Raton, Florida. Local residents were not pleased. An interfaith group put up a sign near the pentagram to announce that "the use of satanic symbols is offensive and harmful to our community's well-being." The pentagram was vandalized several times and ultimately met its demise when someone ran it over with a car. In Michigan, TST has, over several successive years, erected a "Snaketivity" display on the state capitol lawn in Lansing during the holiday season. The display, which consists of a red snake wrapped around a black cross topped by an in-

---

‡   The city of Scottsdale, Arizona, similarly rejected Michelle Shortt's attempt to give an invocation before its city council meeting in 2016, but unlike Phoenix, it has not ended its invocation practice. Accordingly, TST brought suit against the city in early 2018 for religious discrimination.

verted pentagram inscribed with the image of a goat head, has survived unscathed. In 2015, the display, which also boasts a label reading "The Greatest Gift is Knowledge," was described by the Temple as a response to a group of Christians who were planning a "live nativity" event in support of both Jesus Christ and odious presidential candidate Ted Cruz.

And then there is Baphomet.

Oklahoma's constitution, like those of some other states, forbids the use of any public money or property for the support of any church, sect, or religion. But that prohibition did not stop the state's governor in 2012 from signing a law authorizing the erection of a humongous privately donated Ten Commandments monument on the grounds of the state capitol. Many non-Christians regarded the monument as an affront to their beliefs. For the Satanic Temple, however, the monument was also an invitation—an invitation to design and construct its own massive monument and ask that it be displayed at the capitol right alongside the Christian one.

TST's Baphomet is a nine-foot-tall, three-thousand-pound bronze statue of a winged, goat-headed deity that has long been associated with the occult. Two large horns and a torch symbolizing the pursuit of knowledge rise out of the head, which stares straight ahead without expression. Pentagrams adorn both the middle of the head and the deity's throne (the one on the throne is inverted). Although Baphomet is traditionally hermaphroditic and depicted with a woman's breasts, this one is flat-chested because the Temple didn't want to get caught up in any gender-based disputes. The deity's right arm and hand are extended upward, with two fingers pointing to the sky, while the left arm and hand are pointed downward, with two fingers pointing to the ground, following the classic image of Baphomet drawn by a French occultist in the mid-nineteenth century. Bearded, with cloven hooves on crossed legs, the goat-headed figure is flanked by two small children, one boy and one girl, who are gazing up at the deity's head and smiling. On the figure's belly rests a caduceus, two serpents coiled around a staff, symbolizing the "reconciliation of opposites," as TST's Doug Mesner puts it. The monument cost about $100,000, and almost all of that money was crowdfunded. Because Baphomet is sitting down, his lap—like the Atheist bench down in Florida—makes an inviting place to take a seat.

Meanwhile, Oklahoma had installed its Ten Commandments monument not once but twice, since the first one had to be replaced after a Christian guy urinated on it and then ran it over with his car. TST asked the state to install its monument on the grounds of the capitol near the Ten Commandments, but the state refused, and TST readied itself for legal battle. In June 2015, however, the Supreme Court of Oklahoma, in a lawsuit brought by a Baptist minister, held that the Ten Commandments monument violated the state's constitution. A few months later, the stone tablets were removed from state property under cover of darkness. Probably they were installed in the governor's bedroom.

Baphomet, however, lived on. TST moved the monument from Brooklyn, where it was constructed, to Detroit, where the Temple revealed it publicly for the first time at an event in July 2015. Finding a place that was willing to host the unveiling was no easy matter. Seven different venues agreed to let TST use their facilities for the event but then withdrew in the face of virulent protests and threats from Detroit's Christian community. The party eventually took place in an industrial warehouse space and was attended by hundreds of Satanists. Actually getting into the venue was no easy matter either. The Temple sent e-mail messages to ticketholders, instructing them to go to what turned out to be a decoy location, where they were searched and then directed to another location, where the event was actually taking place. Before being admitted, however, attendees had to officially agree to sell their souls to the devil. According to Mesner, "We were thinking that having them sell their souls over to Satan would keep away some of the more superstitious people who would try to undermine the event."

As it happened, the unveiling went fairly smoothly once it was under way. There were protests, of course, at the decoy location, where a busload of Satan-haters sang hymns and one lady sprinkled holy water on people standing in line, but by all accounts the event was a grand and moving affair for those who attended. As Mesner put it: "It was funny to see that contrast between protestors crying because they thought this great evil was being brought to the world, and some of the people during the unveiling with tears in their eyes because they thought this was the culmination of what they've been fighting for for so long finally becoming realized."

At this point, the action moved to Little Rock, Arkansas, where in April 2015, state senator Jason Rapert had sponsored legislation—easily passed—authorizing the placement of a Ten Commandments monument near the state capitol building. With Oklahoma City now in its rearview mirror, TST filed an application in September with the state's Capitol Arts and Grounds Commission to install Baphomet somewhere near the Ten Commandments. In August 2016, in response to a request for further information about the monument and where it might be placed, the Temple filed a more detailed application, asking that Baphomet be situated either within twenty feet to the right or left of the Ten Commandments monument or, alternatively, one foot directly in front of it. Several other groups, including FFRF and Rajan Zed's Universal Society of Hinduism, also asked for permission to erect monuments. At a contentious public meeting held by the Arts and Grounds Commission in December 2016 on the subject of the Ten Commandments monument, many spoke out against the monument on the grounds that it would result either in a lawsuit or in the Satanists coming to town. As one objector put it, "Do you want a Baphomet statue? Because that's how you get a Baphomet statue." The commission, however, moved forward with its plans for the Ten Commandments.

The next month, Doug Mesner traveled to Little Rock for a subcommittee meeting of the Arts and Grounds Commission to provide further details about the Baphomet monument. To reach his destination, he had to pass by a couple of dozen protestors holding signs displaying slogans like "The Virgin Mary triumphs over proud Lucifer. 'She shall crush thy head.' (Gen 3:15)." The subcommittee approved the plans, paving the way for a public meeting in front of the entire commission, which unfortunately never happened because in February 2017, the Arkansas legislature passed a bill requiring that all monuments receive legislative approval before being considered by the commission. Since the chances of the legislature approving a Baphomet monument for the state capitol grounds were precisely 0.0 percent, Baphomet was once again left without a permanent home on public property.

June 2017 saw the erection of the Ten Commandments monument near the Arkansas capitol building, along with a promise by the ACLU to bring suit. The display lasted only one day, however, before the very same

Christian guy who destroyed the monument with his car in Oklahoma did it again in Little Rock. In the aftermath of the incident, more than $50,000 of private money was donated to build another Ten Commandments monument, and in April 2018 Senator Rapert presided over the installation of the new monument. Calling Rapert a "mindless tool for theocratic interests," Doug Mesner (who was there when the new monument went up) promised that a lawsuit would be forthcoming imminently.

So where is Baphomet now? Soon after the monument was unveiled, TST moved it to its national headquarters in Salem, where it was temporarily housed in a shed built by an Amish man who clearly had no idea what the shed was going to be used for. In August 2018, TST brought Baphomet to Little Rock, where the group held a rally to protest Rapert's Ten Commandments monument. After the rally, the Temple brought Baphomet back to Salem and installed the monument inside its headquarters, where it now sits, attracting curious visitors from around the world and waiting for another chance to find its way onto government-owned property.

* * *

One thing the Satanists do not seem to have done (yet, anyway) is to take advantage of the vast amounts of government money that are available for use by religious groups. It would be interesting to see how much controversy TST would cause if it ever applied to receive public funds. In the meantime, however, as chapter 5 illustrates, Muslims who have asked for their rightful share of the public pie have caused plenty enough controversy for everyone.

5

MUSLIMS, MONEY, AND
MIDDLE SCHOOLS

Government Funding of Religion

SCHOOL VOUCHER PROGRAMS OPERATE by giving public money to parents to help them send their children to private schools. Anyone who wasn't aware of such programs before President Donald Trump appointed "Unqualified Betsy" (DeVos) to be the secretary of education probably knows about them now. The grants are designed to allow poor parents who would otherwise have no choice but to enroll their kids in poorly performing public schools to send them instead to a better-performing private school. The debate over whether these programs actually improve education is, of course, enormous and substantial. Opponents contend, among other things, that vouchers take money away from public schools and make already troubled school systems even worse, to the detriment of most students.

What is particularly important to the subject of this book, however, is that typically the set of private schools from which voucher recipients can choose includes religious schools, primarily Christian ones. Although many legal scholars have argued that using public money to fund religious schools violates the First Amendment, the Supreme Court decided in 2002 in a case from Cleveland that as long as the parents get to decide where to spend the money, and as long as the schools they can choose from are formally "neutral" with respect to religion (meaning that both religious and non-religious schools can participate), then voucher programs do not violate the

Constitution. This is true even if, as was the case in Cleveland, almost all the schools receiving money from the program are Christian.

Although the Court's decision did not, as many had predicted, lead to a tidal wave of new voucher programs being adopted across the nation, several states and localities have considered such programs over the past decade and a half, and a handful have adopted them. Some lawmakers in a couple of these places, however, have hesitated to support vouchers for a unique and troubling reason—not because they were worried that vouchers could harm students or harm public schools or promote religion, but rather because they might end up promoting one specific religion, namely Islam.

New Orleans, for example, started a voucher program in 2008. A few years later, the Louisiana legislature was debating whether to extend that program to the entire state. The bill was set to pass easily until it was reported that a small Muslim school called the Islamic School of Greater New Orleans expected to participate in the program by accepting thirty-eight voucher students. When this became news, several Louisiana legislators suddenly changed their view about voucher schools and withdrew their support for the program. *Wait a second*, these people basically asked. *Christianity isn't the only religion with schools?*

State representative Kenneth Havard, for instance, said that he would not vote for any program that "will fund Islamic teaching," observing that he wouldn't "go back home and explain to my people that I supported this." Another state representative feared that "it'll be the Church of Scientology next year." Taking the cake for Islamophobic idiocy, though, was Republican state representative Valarie Hodges, who declared, "I actually support funding for teaching the fundamentals of America's Founding Fathers' religion, which is Christianity, in public schools or private schools [but] we need to insure that it does not open the door to fund radical Islam schools. There are a thousand Muslim schools that have sprung up recently [and] I do not support using public funds for teaching Islam anywhere in Louisiana." In the wake of these comments, the Islamic School of Greater New Orleans, for unreported reasons, withdrew its request to participate in the voucher program. The program then passed the legislature by a 51–49 margin.

Louisiana, moreover, is not the only place where support for voucher programs threatened to turn sour when lawmakers realized that Islamic schools would be included. In Tennessee, where the legislature has been unable to enact vouchers, several lawmakers have made comments similar to the ones in Louisiana. One state senator, for instance, voiced his "considerable concern" that public money might end up funding schools that teach the Qur'an; another lawmaking bozo named Bill Ketron, who had earlier expressed concern that a mop sink installed outside the House men's room might have been built for Muslims to wash their feet, referred to the funding of Muslim schools as "an issue we must address" and openly wondered whether the program could be finessed to exclude them. (No.)

Writers on both the left and the right have invoked the specter of radical Islamic terrorism as a potential problem with the public funding of Islamic schools. An article that appeared in the left-leaning *Mother Jones* magazine soon after the 2016 election suggested that Vice President Mike Pence's support for voucher programs might run directly counter to his fear of Islam, citing the fact that a Muslim school in his home state of Indiana received vouchers. Piling on, the article noted that in 2013, a Muslim teenager who had spent eight weeks as a student at the school was indicted for supporting terrorism. More predictably, an Islamophobic organization in Tennessee published an anti-voucher newsletter titled *State Funded School Vouchers Support Teaching Hate for Kaffirs*, in which, among other things, the group noted that students in Islamic schools will undoubtedly recite the first chapter of the Qur'an as part of their daily prayers and then wondered: "Who in their right mind would want to pay for *this???*"* The newsletter, which was posted on a variety of anti-Islam websites, including ones called Creeping Sharia and Gates of Vienna, also pointed out, as a way of scaring its readers, that when North Carolina implemented its school voucher program, the largest consumer of vouchers was an Islamic school in the Raleigh-Durham area.

Wow, I thought, reading these accounts. Who knew that Islamic elementary and middle schools could be so dangerous??? I booked a flight to North Carolina to see for myself.

---

* Apoplectic triple italicized question marks appear in original.

* * *

The law concerning whether and when the government can give money or other types of aid to religion is a bit more complicated than the other areas of law I've talked about so far in this book, but it's not nearly as complicated as it used to be. For about fifty years—starting in 1947 with the case of *Everson v. Board of Education* and lasting until just after the turn of the millennium—the Court decided probably two dozen important cases sorting out what kinds of government aid to religion were okay and what kinds were not. These cases were a hot mess, as the kids say, because they tried to draw subtle distinctions between government programs (usually involving education in some way) that seemed to be very similar.

For instance, in *Everson*, the Court held that a state could include religious schools in its public busing program, so that kids who went to religious schools as well as those who went to public schools could take advantage of free public transportation, but in a case a couple of decades later the Court held that states couldn't provide free busing to religious school students for field trips. According to the Court, the two situations were different because field trips are related to the school's curriculum, while buses to and from school itself are not. Similarly, although the Court held early on that states could provide religious schools with textbooks on secular subjects free of charge, it later held that states could not do the same with secular instructional materials like computers or filmstrips, because these items would be more likely than books to be diverted to religious purposes. In yet another dicey sequence of cases, the Court held that a state could send public employees into religious schools to provide speech, hearing, and psychological services, but could not provide personnel to teach classes in those schools, even if those classes were in secular subjects like math or reading.

Although these distinctions struck many scholars and observers as silly, it is not hard to understand why the Court felt it needed to make them. Providing government aid to religion may be harmful in a variety of ways—it risks promoting some religions over others, involves the government in religious affairs, and encourages religions to compete with one another for government largesse—but in the complex modern world, where the government naturally reaches into so much of ordinary life, it is also to some degree inevitable. For example, the government provides police, fire, trash, and sewage services to all citizens and institutions, but nobody in their right mind thinks that the government should withhold these services from churches or other religious entities. Is the fire department really supposed to stand by and watch a temple burn because people are praying inside? Indeed, if a state or town excluded religion from basic services, most people would probably feel like the government was unacceptably discriminating *against* religion.

Government programs that provide aid of some sort to religious education raise the same problem. Is providing math books to religious schools as part of a program of providing math books to all schools analogous to providing police and fire protection to those schools? Or does it go too far in promoting the core mission of the religious schools such that the harms simply become too great? The Court in *Everson*, while devoting a good amount of space to the potential dangers of providing government aid to religion, ultimately concluded that whatever benefit the government provided to religion by offering free busing to religious schools was incidental to its legitimate interest in helping kids get a good education. The distinctions that the Court tried to draw over the next fifty years or so represent the good-faith effort of the justices to distinguish what types of aid were particularly dangerous from those for which the benefit to religion was incidental to the overall legitimate public aims of the government.

In any event, the era of fine distinctions has come to an end. In two cases— *Mitchell v. Helms* from 2000 and *Zelman v. Simmons-Harris* from 2002—the Supreme Court has greatly clarified and simplified the law concerning public aid to religion. At this point, it is probably fair to say that you can understand about 90 percent of the current legal doctrine in this area by grasping two basic concepts. The first is that for government aid to religious individuals or institutions to be valid, the religious recipients must be part of a *formally neutral class of recipients* that includes both religious and non-religious individuals or institutions. The second concept is that aid that goes directly from the government to the religious recipient (*direct aid*) differs from aid that goes first to some private individual or entity who then chooses to funnel it to a religious recipient (*indirect aid*). As we'll see, the Court is more wary of direct aid to religion than it is of indirect aid.

So, first: At a bare minimum, if a government program that aids religion is to be constitutional, the religious recipients of the aid must be part of a formally neutral class of recipients, i.e., a class defined without respect to religion. This means that the government may not administer a program that provides money or other types of aid *only* to religious entities. For example, a state could not create a voucher program that included only religious schools or give textbooks free of charge only to religious schools or create a historic preservation fund that could be used only to restore religious buildings or give a thousand dollars to every soup kitchen run by a religious organization but not to other soup kitchens. Rather, at a minimum, the government would have to design its voucher program to include both religious and non-religious schools, give books to both religious and secular schools, make historic preservation funds available to restore both religious and non-religious buildings, and give its thousand dollars to all soup kitchens, regardless of whether they are run by religious organizations. The point here is to ensure a certain formal level of government neutrality toward religion, with the assumption being that a program that aids only religion promotes religion over non-religion, while one that aids religion as part of a class defined without regard to religion is simply treating religious entities like everybody else.

The second concept is the distinction between direct and indirect aid. If the money or other aid (books, computers, hammers, buckets of seaweed salad, whatever) goes from the government straight to the religious recipients, then it is considered direct aid. If, however, the money or other aid goes to some individual or entity other than the final recipient, and then that individual or entity decides where to send it, and the individual or entity decides to send the aid to a religious recipient, that is considered indirect aid. School voucher programs are the paradigmatic example of indirect aid. The government makes a certain amount of money available to parents in the form of a voucher (usually the statute defines which parents are eligible for the voucher on the basis of where they live and how much money they earn), and then the parents decide where to spend the voucher. The set of schools that the parents can choose from is determined by the government and must of course (pursuant to the first concept) include both religious and non-religious schools. The Court considers this aid to be indirect because it is ultimately the decision of the intermediary parents, rather than the government itself, that determines whether the money goes to a religious recipient.

The distinction is important because the Court has applied different constitutional tests to evaluate direct aid to religion and indirect aid to religion. Because direct aid is not mediated by any intervening individual and instead flows directly from the government to religion, the Court has been stricter in policing direct aid than indirect aid. The rule is that direct aid to religious entities may not be used by those entities to promote their religious mission.

The key modern case is *Mitchell v. Helms*. That complicated case involved a challenge to how federal educational funds were being spent and used in Jefferson Parish, Louisiana. The federal grant program at issue distributed money to state and local educational agencies for the purposes of purchasing educational materials and equipment and required those agencies to distribute the materials and equipment to both public and private schools within their jurisdictions. Jefferson Parish used its funds under the program to provide schools within its district with "library books, computers, and computer software, and also slide and movie projectors, overhead projectors, television sets, tape recorders, VCR's, projection screens, laboratory equipment, maps, globes, filmstrips, slides, and cassette recordings."[†] The parish distributed these items to its public schools as well as its private schools. Of the forty-six private schools in the district, forty-one of them were religious. Under the terms of the federal grant program, religious schools receiving materials were required to use them only for secular purposes.

The plaintiffs who brought the challenge claimed that by giving instructional materials directly to religious schools, the parish had violated the Establishment Clause as interpreted by the Court in several earlier opinions decided during the era of fine distinctions. Although the plaintiffs conceded

---

† Now might be a good time for anyone reading this who is under the age of forty to Google "VCR's," "overhead projectors," and "filmstrips."

that the program restricted the use of materials to secular purposes, they nonetheless claimed that those materials were "reasonably divertible" to religious uses, and that this feature rendered the aid unconstitutional. The Court disagreed and upheld the program, but like many decisions in the church/state area, several opinions have to be carefully read together to understand what law actually comes out of the case. Although all the justices agreed that the aid was distributed to a formally neutral class of recipients, they disagreed strongly on whether it mattered that religious schools might divert the aid from secular to religious purposes. For simplicity's sake, I'll pretend I'm a marketing executive and use bullet points to explain the different opinions:

- Justice Thomas wrote an opinion for four justices basically saying that so long as the aid itself was not religious in nature, it did not matter one whit whether it had been diverted to religious uses or could be diverted to religious uses.‡

- Justice O'Connor wrote a concurring opinion for just herself and Justice Breyer saying that although it would be unconstitutional for the religious schools to divert the aid to religious uses, there was really no evidence that such diversion had occurred in Jefferson Parish.

- Justice Souter wrote a dissenting opinion for three justices saying that the aid was unconstitutional because it was "highly susceptible" to being diverted for religious uses.

Notice that no opinion got a majority of the justices to sign on. When that happens, the rule is that the narrowest opinion supporting the ultimate judgment in the case prevails. Here, that means that Justice O'Connor's concurring opinion essentially becomes the law. Key to her analysis was that the grant program involved direct aid. In her view, when the

---

‡ The case would have been different for these justices if the aid were explicitly religious in nature--for instance, if it involved giving religious books to schools. It also might have been different if the aid were given purely in the form of cash.

government gives direct aid to religious entities, those entities cannot use that aid for religious purposes. As of this writing, that remains the state of the law.§

One of the big questions following the Court's decision in *Mitchell* was whether programs involving indirect aid would be subject to the same type of restriction. The Court resolved that question in the negative in the 2002 case of *Zelman v. Simmons-Harris*, which upheld Cleveland's school voucher program against constitutional attack.

The facts of the case were complicated, but these are the key points, somewhat simplified. Cleveland's public schools were performing so poorly in the mid-1990s that a federal court placed the school district under the control of the State of Ohio. Ohio then enacted a voucher program applicable to the school district of every city within the state that had been ordered by a court to be controlled by the state—in other words, any city named "Cleveland." The program provided a voucher of roughly $2,200 to any family in the city whose income was 200 percent or more below the poverty line (and a slightly smaller voucher for other families). The family could use that voucher to pay for a significant percentage of the tuition of any private school that chose to participate in the voucher program. In the 1999–2000 school year (the year under review by the Court), fifty-six schools chose to participate in the program; forty-six of those, or 82 percent, were religious schools, almost all of them Christian. About 3,700

---

§   It should be noted, though, that this restriction is hanging by a thread. Justice O'Connor retired in 2006 and was replaced by Samuel Alito, who is more solicitous of religion than his predecessor was. In the recent case of *Trinity Lutheran Church of Columbia, Inc. v. Comer*, decided in June 2017, the Court held that the State of Missouri could not exclude a church from receiving aid in the form of a grant to purchase a rubber playground surface made out of recycled tires. In a footnote, the Court wrote: "This case involves express discrimination based on religious identity with respect to playground resurfacing. We do not address religious uses of funding or other forms of discrimination." Justices Thomas and Gorsuch, however, refused to join this specific footnote (it's true—they joined the entire opinion, except for one footnote!), and Justice Gorsuch wrote a concurring opinion in which he criticized the distinction in the Court's footnote. If the Court were to reconsider *Mitchell v. Helms* (or a case presenting similar facts) today, it might very well decide that even direct aid can be used for religious purposes.

students used a voucher to attend one of those fifty-six private schools, and 96 percent of those students attended a religious school, although by no means always a school of the same denomination as their parents. In addition to these private schools and the regular public schools in the Cleveland district, the city also ran about twenty magnet schools and had approved ten charter schools. As public schools, these magnet and charter schools could not be affiliated with any religion.

The plaintiffs argued that Cleveland's voucher program violated the Establishment Clause, but the Court, in a 5–4 decision, disagreed. The majority opinion was written by Chief Justice Rehnquist and joined by Justices O'Connor, Scalia, Kennedy, and Thomas. In Rehnquist's view, "where a government aid program is neutral with respect to religion, and provides assistance directly to a broad class of citizens who, in turn, direct government aid to religious schools wholly as a result of their own genuine and independent choice," the program is constitutional. Since Cleveland's voucher program involved "true private choice" that was "neutral in all respects toward religion," the decision to uphold the program was straightforward. On the question of neutrality, Rehnquist concluded that the voucher program at issue provided "no financial incentives that skew the program toward religious schools."

Justice Souter's dissent, which was joined by Justices Stevens, Ginsburg, and Breyer, argued that by burdening the freedom of conscience of nonbelievers, corrupting religion, and causing social conflict, the voucher program violated "every objective underlying the prohibition of religious establishment." Specifically, Souter objected to Rehnquist's conclusion that nothing in the program skewed it toward religious schools. Surely, Souter suggested, "something is influencing choices in a way that aims the money in a religious direction," since 96 percent of the students in the program ended up going to religious schools. Among other things, Souter wondered whether the fact that the roughly $2,000 voucher that the state provided to parents was playing that role, since the average tuition of Catholic schools at the time was $1,600 and the average tuition of non-religious private schools was closer to $4,000. In response to this point, the majority countered that the percentage of students who ended up attending religious schools was irrelevant, since it was most likely a result of the fact that most private schools in Cleveland just happened to be religious schools.

Additionally, Justice Rehnquist thought that the 96 percent figure was inaccurate because it did not take into account all of the non-religious schools that parents could choose for their kids. According to Rehnquist, an accurate percentage should have included in the denominator not only the private non-religious schools participating in the voucher program, but also the city's public charter and magnet schools. Including the nearly 15,000 students attending those schools, Rehnquist wrote, "drops the percentage enrolled in religious schools from 96% to 20%." Justice Souter went ballistic on this point (well, ballistic for a Supreme Court justice), arguing that including public schools in the denominator "confuses choice in spending scholarships with choice from the entire menu of possible educational placements" and would mean that even a voucher program that included no private non-religious schools would be unconstitutional. In a separate concurrence, Justice O'Connor added that the $8.2 million that the voucher program sent to Cleveland's religious schools "pales in comparison to the amount of funds that federal, state, and local governments already provide religious institutions" through tax exemptions, tax deductions, and other government programs, a point that Justice Souter described as "no less irrelevant" than the point made by Justice Rehnquist.¶

In separate dissenting opinions, both Justice Stevens and Justice Breyer warned about the potential for religious divisiveness created by the Court's decision. Pointing to the Balkans, Northern Ireland, and the Middle East, Justice Stevens observed, "Whenever we remove a brick from the wall that was designed to separate religion and government, we increase the risk of religious strife and weaken the foundation of our democracy." More specifically, Justice Breyer argued that voucher programs are particularly dangerous given the importance of primary education to religious believers: "Why will different religions not become concerned about, and seek to influence, the criteria used to channel [billions of dollars] to religious schools? Why will they not want to examine the implementation of the

¶   The point might have been irrelevant, but it's certainly true. Churches and other religious institutions probably save at least $70 billion annually by not having to pay taxes.

programs that provide this money? . . . If so, just how is the State to resolve the resulting controversies without provoking legitimate fears of the kinds of religious favoritism that, in so religiously diverse a Nation, threaten social dissension?" The majority rejected these substantial concerns out of hand, noting that "we quite rightly have rejected the claim that some speculative potential for divisiveness bears on the constitutionality of educational aid programs."

* * *

Beginning with the "charitable choice" legislation of the mid-1990s and continuing with even greater force through the "faith-based initiatives" of the Bush, Obama, and Trump administrations, the government has funneled billions of dollars directly to religious organizations that provide social services such as substance abuse assistance, soup kitchens, food banks, and job training to needy individuals. Although as direct aid, this money cannot constitutionally be used for religious purposes like proselytizing, worship, or religious education, separationist critics argue that lots of the money does end up supporting religious activities, either because religious organizations defy the legal limits on use of the money and get away with it (monitoring the actual use of so much money is, after all, nearly impossible) or because the injection of cash for social services frees up money originally allocated by religious groups for those services to be used for other things (money is, after all, largely fungible) or because providing social services as a religious organization is in fact a religious activity (determining what activities performed by an organization function as religious is, after all, a difficult task).

Figuring out how much of this money has been given to minority religious organizations as opposed to Christian ones is difficult, but it seems clear that it is but a tiny fraction of the total amount spent by the government. Databases document which groups have gotten how much money from which government agencies, but even though I have looked at some of these, I am hardly confident that the figure I could tell you would be anything close to an exact amount or percentage of money that has flowed to minority groups, if for no other reason than that generally the databases list only the receiving group's name and not its religious affiliation. A few clearly religious groups representing minorities have received large amounts of aid, including Islamic centers in North Carolina and Missouri and Buddhist foundations in California and Massachusetts, but even a quick scan of the data indicates what should hardly be surprising—namely, that almost all the recipients whose names are recognizable as religious have some affiliation with Christianity. It is, of course, impossible to say how much of this aid, whether to Christian or non-Christian groups, has in fact been used for religious purposes in violation of the First Amendment.

As with the voucher program controversies in Louisiana and Tennessee described at the beginning of the chapter, when powerful Christians realize that government money might go to "weird" minority religions, they sometimes freak out. For instance, Jim Towey, a Roman Catholic who directed the White House Office of Faith-Based and Community Initiatives for four years in the Bush administration, was once asked if Pagan groups would be eligible for government money just like any other religious group. His response: "I haven't run into a pagan faith-based group yet, much less a pagan group that cares for the poor! Once you make it clear to any applicant that public money must go to public purposes and can't be used to promote ideology, the fringe groups lose interest. Helping the poor is tough work, and only those with loving hearts seem drawn to it." Similarly, Pat Robertson once worried publicly that "such groups as the Unification Church, the Hare Krishnas, and the Church of Scientology could all become financial beneficiaries of the proposal to extend eligibility for government grants to religious charities." "I hate," he added, "to find myself on the side of the Anti-Defamation League."

Lo and behold, both the Unification Church and the Church of Scientology have received federal funds, and in both instances, the media have jumped all over them. In 2004, the *San Francisco Chronicle* reported that "at least four longtime operatives of [Reverend Sun Myung Moon's] Unification Church are on the federal payroll or getting government grants in the administration's Healthy Marriage Initiative and other 'faith-based' programs." One of those grants, in the amount of $475,000, went from the Department of Health and Human Resources to "Free Teens," a pro-abstinence education group run by Richard Panzer, a member of the Unification Church. Another, more complicated arrangement involved a $365,000 grant from

President Bush's Compassion Capital Fund to a conservative think tank that partnered with an organization called the California State Healthy Marriage and Responsible Fatherhood Initiative, which ran a marriage education training seminar in partnership with the University of Bridgeport, a school owned by a Unification Church–affiliated group. Leading the seminar was Josephine Hauer, a graduate of Reverend Moon's Unification Theological Seminary and former "director of marriage education"** at the University of Bridgeport. Although both Hauer and Panzer denied that they used the government funds to promote the Unification Church or its teachings, Americans United was not so sure. According to Barry Lynn, AU's former executive director, "Moon has been a big backer of the faith-based initiative. But it's beyond belief that you can have the University of Bridgeport issuing marriage education certificates and claim that is secular."

Meanwhile, in the fall of 2010, the U.S. Department of Defense made a nearly $635 million grant to an entity known as the Gulf War Veterans Research Program to conduct a study on a detoxification treatment long championed by the Church of Scientology. The treatment program, which combines aerobic exercise, extended sessions in an extremely hot sauna, and the ingestion of high amounts of niacin, was developed initially by Scientologist founder L. Ron Hubbard in the 1970s and has been used by countless Scientologists and non-Scientologists to battle drug addiction and other afflictions ever since. Although many patients claim to have benefited from the regime (they say they can feel and see the toxins being secreted from their skin), critics of Scientology have been highly skeptical, and as of 2010 no objective, rigorous scientific studies had ever been performed to evaluate the treatment's efficacy.††

** *What??!*

†† An article in the *Daily Beast* describes the treatment program like this: "The subjects come in and do cardio for 30 minutes, followed by two to four hours of sweating in a sauna, a mega-dose of vitamins, especially niacin, (one participant said by the end she was drinking two large canning jars of vitamins per day), and a few spoonfuls of peanut oil, to replace the 'toxic fat' with 'healthy fat.'" As for the toxins being excreted from the skin, the *Daily Beast* article continues: "'I was going to be done today,' [Participant No. 29] tells Crystal Grant, the project's affable coordinator. 'But . . . I had some more junk come out of my legs. Some black stuff. So I'm going to do one more day and see if I can clean it all out.'"

The Gulf War Veterans Research Program, which also received funding from an organization chaired by famous Scientologist and former Sweathog John Travolta, studied the effects of the Scientologist detoxification protocol on a group of veterans suffering from Gulf War syndrome, a condition that the Veterans Administration defines as "a cluster of medically unexplained chronic conditions" that often includes headaches, fatigue, and memory problems. The primary investigator of the study was a professor of environmental health at the University of Albany named David Carpenter, who, although not a Scientologist himself, is known for studying controversial subjects; according to Carpenter, it was his work on the purported dangers of "electromagnetic hypersensitivity" from cell phones and power lines that "convinced the Scientologists to approach him." Others who worked on the study, which took place in the basement of a building in Annapolis, Maryland, were practicing Scientologists, such as Kathleen Kerr, a lecturer at the University of Toronto who formerly appeared in church advertisements, and a guy named Joe, described by Carpenter as a "die-hard Scientologist," who was responsible for determining how much niacin each subject should receive. Although participants claim that they were not proselytized by the Church of Scientology in any way during the study, former church members have argued that the church will use the study to promote its religion, and experts on study design have critiqued the involvement of Kerr and other Scientologists in the study as creating a risk of bias.[‡‡]

* * *

Public funding of Islamic institutions—in the forms of both direct aid and indirect aid—has periodically raised hackles. Critics have pointed, for example, to the millions of dollars received by the Islamic Center of Greater Kansas City from the Department of Agriculture over the years

---

[‡‡] The Krishnas, too, have received plenty of government funding over the years for running halfway houses, homeless shelters, and addiction centers. As the *New York Times* commented at the very beginning of George W. Bush's presidency: "The unusual collaboration between government agencies and a religious group that depicts God as a baby-faced boy with blue skin offers a glimpse of the challenges ahead for President Bush's initiative to expand government support for social service programs run by religious organizations." Indeed.

as particularly concerning. These critics have taken issue with the fact that the center is owned by the North American Islamic Trust, which they claim is linked in various ways to the financing of terrorist activities. More interesting, though, has been the reaction of the Muslim community to federal funding grants for combating terrorism.

For example, the Countering Violent Extremism program, initiated during the Obama administration and administered by the Department of Homeland Security, was originally styled to fight both foreign and domestic radicalization by providing large grants to institutions that were well suited to carrying out such efforts. The program was always somewhat controversial among Islamic institutions, but this skepticism took a great leap forward after Donald Trump was elected president in 2016. In the wake of the election, at least four Muslim organizations rejected grants totaling more than $2 million, claiming that they "cannot in good conscience accept" grants from an administration that promotes "hate, fear, uncertainty and even worse, an unofficial war on Muslim-Americans and immigrants." The largest of these awards was an $800,000 grant to a private Islamic graduate school in California named Bayan Claremont, which had applied for the money to create a project to "improve inter-religious cooperation, civic engagement, and social justice."

Given the histrionic yammering of those legislators who have opposed inclusion of Islamic schools in their state voucher programs (recall Louisiana representative Valarie Hodges, who claimed that "a thousand Muslim schools . . . have sprung up recently"), one might be surprised to learn that in fact the government is not emptying its coffers to promote the teaching of Islam. Indeed, according to the Islamic Schools League of America, an organization founded in 1998 to facilitate communication, networking, and information sharing among Islamic schools in the United States, only about three hundred such schools exist, and of those, only a few participate in voucher programs.[§§] Still, though, it is true that a handful of

---

§§ According to a superb comprehensive study conducted by the *Huffington Post*, about one percent of voucher schools identify as Muslim. Two percent identify as Jewish. The rest of the religious voucher schools (which make up about 75 percent of all voucher schools) are Christian or Catholic, except for about five schools that use a curriculum developed by L. Ron Hubbard.

schools that directly promote Islam receive government funds. A couple of them are located in the Raleigh-Durham area of North Carolina, which is where I went to learn what I could about these allegedly dangerous (!!!) elementary schools.

The Al-Iman K–8 school in Raleigh was founded in 1992 and currently serves about three hundred students, sixty-five of whom were using vouchers during the 2016–17 school year (each voucher is for about $4,200 and covers most of the cost of tuition). The school is known as the "Home of the Honeybees," which is a reference to a passage in the Qur'an, and the office door of Mussarut Jabeen, the school's dynamic principal, has a sign on it that says "Queen Bee." Jabeen had been extraordinarily kind and inviting when I asked if I could come visit her school, so when I arrived at her office on the third floor of the Raleigh Islamic Center, where most of the school's classes are held (some are held in a small building next door), I was feeling at ease and excited to be there.

I showed up during a break between classes, so the kids were making a ruckus in the hallway outside the office, boisterous boys laughing and yakking about their cell phones and whatever else tweens talk about these days. Jabeen took me on a little tour around the school; apart from some Arabic on the walls and teachers wearing headscarves, it looked like basically any other small elementary/middle school in the country. We went into a class of third graders, who all recognized Jabeen and greeted her in Arabic. She asked the teacher what they were doing, and the teacher replied, "We're talking about what we'll be when we grow up." Jabeen asked the class if anyone wanted to be a teacher, and one girl raised her hand. A couple of seconds passed before a boy declared that he would "like to be a boy teacher." Another classroom we peeked into had "flexible seating," with all sorts of different options—not only regular wooden chairs, but beanbags, rugs, and one of those big bouncy rubber balls you see at gyms. Jabeen explained to me that the kids earned the right to choose where they wanted to sit by behaving properly. As we walked from the secondary building back to the Islamic Center, a group of sweating and tired second graders were returning from a gym class. Jabeen greeted them with encouragement and hugs. This is clearly a principal who adores her students, and whose students adore her right back.

When we had settled in Jabeen's office again, I asked her what she thought of middle schoolers. As the parent of a teenager myself, I can't imagine a more difficult job than running a school full of those hormone-addled whirlybirds, but Jabeen said that she has a special interest in kids of that age and loves getting to know them and nurturing them. Wow. She told me that there's "no child who cannot learn" and that she focuses on each child's growth—academic, social, and human—rather than on benchmarks of accomplishment. She admitted that she faces many challenges, everything from fidget spinners in the classrooms ("they're contagious!") to more-pressing concerns, like how to run a school with limited resources, but it's clear that she is devoted to getting the very best for her students. Sometimes you just have to think outside the box. For example, Jabeen explained how for an entire year she sold pizza slices each Friday afternoon so she could get enough money to purchase a Chromebook for every student in the school.

I hadn't expected to talk much about Finland on my trip to an Islamic school in North Carolina, but that's the great thing about actually getting out there and meeting new people—you never know what's going to happen. About a year earlier, Jabeen had traveled as part of an educational trip with some other teachers to Finland and had returned with a slew of innovative ideas from what she referred to as the "Finnish model" of education. The flexible seating plan that I had seen in her classroom was one of those ideas, but just a small example of the overall approach, which emphasizes empowerment of both students and teachers. According to Jabeen, seeing the Finnish model up close encouraged her to trust in her teachers and to free them, to the extent possible, from having to teach to standardized tests. When she returned from her trip, she met personally with every teacher in the school to find out more about who they were and what they had done (and wanted to do) in the classroom. Impressed, I asked her whether she thought she was unique among principals of Islamic schools, and she agreed that she probably is, but that through her work with the Islamic Schools League of America (she serves on the board of directors for the organization), which runs a "leadership retreat" every year, she hopes to spread her ideas to other leaders in Islamic education around the country.

I wanted to understand the role of Islam in the education that the school provides its students, so I asked specifically about how religion is incorporated into the school day. Jabeen explained that in addition to the typical secular subjects taught everywhere, Al-Iman also requires all its students to study the Qur'an as well as Arabic as a foreign language. The goal of the Arabic program is in part to help students understand the Qur'an. Indeed, the religious teaching is integrated throughout the curriculum. Teachers incorporate religious materials into their secular lessons, and students engage in interdisciplinary projects that bring together not only several secular subjects, but Muslim teachings as well. The school emphasizes teaching students about Muslim heritage and history, exposing them to prominent historic and contemporary Islamic figures in science, language arts, and other fields. Students celebrate Muslim holidays and pray several times a day, including meeting together for prayer after lunch in the capacious community mosque downstairs from the classrooms.

Community service is also a critical aspect of the school's mission. Students regularly collect food and other supplies to help hungry families and the homeless. The school has always focused on helping others, but this calling has become more urgent and poignant in the wake of the tragic events of February 10, 2015, when a hate-filled neighbor killed three former Al-Iman students execution style in their Chapel Hill apartment. I had no idea about these murders when I planned my trip to visit the school, but as it turns out, the tragedy has now become central to Al-Iman's identity.

Deah Barakat, a twenty-three-year-old dental student at the University of North Carolina, lived with his wife, Yusor Abu-Salha, a recent graduate of North Carolina State University, who was also planning to attend dental school at UNC, in a small complex known as Finley Forest. Ever since Barakat had moved to the apartment in 2013, he had run into trouble with a white neighbor in his mid-forties named Craig Hicks, a gun-owning Atheist who lived with his wife and was studying at a local community college to become a paralegal.

By all accounts, Hicks was completely obsessed with the parking situation at Finley Forest; although all units were assigned one parking space, with the remaining five spaces free for anyone to use, Hicks insisted that the space next to his assigned one was to be used only by his wife. On numerous occasions, Hicks came over to Barakat's apartment to emphasize this arrangement. Although Barakat knew that he had as much right to use the contested space as anyone else, he went out of his way to acquiesce to Hicks's demands, even going so far as to draw up a map for friends who might visit the apartment, directing them to park on the street rather in the parking lot. After Barakat and Abu-Salha became engaged and Abu-Salha started spending more time at the apartment, Hicks's agitation increased. On one occasion, after Abu-Salha and some friends had spent a few hours playing the board game Risk in the apartment, Hicks came over to tell them they had been too loud. He pulled up his shirt to reveal a gun in his waistband. Abu-Salha was frightened and convinced that Hicks disapproved of her religion and her headscarf. "Daddy," she told her father, Mohammad, not long before she was murdered, "we feel he hates us for who we are and how we look."

At about five o'clock in the evening of February 10, police responded to a 911 call placed by a woman who had heard gunshots and screams coming from the complex and found Barakat, Abu-Salha, and Abu-Salha's sister Razan, who was visiting the couple, murdered in the apartment. Both women had been shot in the head at close range; Barakat's body was riddled with bullets. Only about an hour passed before Craig Hicks turned himself in to the police. In the weeks and months following the incident, debate raged over the motive for the killings. Hicks's wife claimed that the murders were "related to a longstanding parking dispute that my husband had with the neighbors." The families of the victims and a host of others claimed that the murders were clearly hate crimes. Supporters of the hate-crimes theory pointed not only to the fact that Hicks was a militant Atheist whose Facebook page was filled with anti-religion rants, but also to the fact that on the day of the killings, none of the victims had been parked in the disputed parking space supposedly reserved for Hicks's wife. Although Hicks was indicted on three counts of first-degree murder and will be facing a death-penalty prosecution, no hate-crime charges were ever officially brought, and the U.S. attorney in charge of investigating the case for the federal government concluded that the murders were "not part of a targeted campaign against Muslims."

The outpouring of support and love for the victims and their families in the wake of the murders was immense. Thousands of people attended a vigil on the campus of the University of North Carolina on the day following the incident, and even more attended the public funeral on February 12 at North Carolina State University. Memorial services and vigils were held on university campuses across the country and in cities around the world. The Twitter hashtag #MuslimLivesMatter went viral. Steph Curry, the National Basketball Association's most valuable player and Barakat's favorite player, wore sneakers honoring the victims during the league's all-star weekend and then sent the shoes to Barakat's family. North Carolina State established scholarships known as the Our Three Winners Fund, incorporating the phrase of praise for the three victims that became widely used after the murders. Donations to a fund for providing dental care to Syrians in Turkey, which Barakat had established before his death, jumped from $3,000 to more than $300,000 within days.

Despite the unimaginable anguish felt by members of Barakat's and Abu Salah's families, the message that they sought to convey to the world after the murders was one of peace and love. At the initial vigil at UNC, Barakat's mother, Layla, told the crowd, "He died of a hate crime and his legacy is never hate. You don't respond back by hating the other. You respond back by love. By peace, by mercy." At the events held at North Carolina State, Barakat's sister, Suzanne, said, "The message that we want to share is to spread love, spread awareness because these people were nothing but love and kindness." In an article published in *Time* magazine written by Barakat's brother, Farris, and Abu-Salha's father, Mohammad, the two bereaved family members insisted that their loved ones were killed by hate, claiming that "citing the hateful murder of Our Three Winners as an 'ongoing parking dispute' is like re-telling the story of Rosa Park[s]'s civil rights struggle as an 'ongoing dispute over a bus seat.'" Still, though, the two wrote that the answer to hate is not more hate but rather love and understanding: "The most important action we can all take now is to get to know our neighbors. By knowing one another we can begin to overcome hate and to prevent future tragedies like the one that befell our family. . . . We know that we must not fight hate with hate. Instead, we will carry their legacy of love against hate."

It seems clear that Al-Iman and its principal, Mussarut Jabeen, helped contribute significantly to the development of these amazing three people. All of them were students at the school when they were young, and all had had Jabeen as a teacher. The relationship between the victims and their former teacher remained close throughout the years. As Margaret Talbot wrote in her story about the murders for the *New Yorker*, "Although Barakat was twenty-three, he still stopped by his old grammar school—Al-Iman, a private institution in Raleigh that offered 'an Islamic environment'—to say hello to Mussarut Jabeen, the principal. Jabeen is on the short side, and Barakat sometimes greeted her by walking up behind her and gently placing his hand on her head. She was delighted to learn that Barakat was planning to marry Abu-Salha, another Al-Iman graduate. 'You will be together for the rest of your lives, *inshallah*,' Jabeen said."

The year before the shootings, when the NPR-affiliated oral-history project StoryCorps came to Raleigh, Yusor Abu-Salha interviewed Jabeen for it. In the course of the discussion between the teacher and her former pupil, Abu-Salha recalled one of the foundational lessons she had learned from Jabeen. "I still remember, in third grade, when we asked for something," Abu-Salha told Jabeen, "you used to say, 'Don't put your hand like this.' You would have your hand facing downwards as if you're taking something from someone. . . . And then you'd flip your hand over and you'd open your hand upward as, you know, a giving gesture. You know, be giving, open, compassionate." Abu-Salha lived that lesson, spending an extended period during the summer before her death volunteering at a dental clinic for Syrian refugees in Turkey. In another exchange, Abu-Salha asked her former teacher what she would tell the world if she had its attention. Jabeen responded: "Live in peace. . . . Make this world a place where everybody has the right to live and we don't fight over our differences but learn to accept our differences." "Sister Jabeen, I love hearing from you," Abu Salha responded. "You always have the right thing to say, the right answers."

Later in the interview, in a passage that is painful to read in light of what happened to her, Abu-Salha continued:

Growing up in America has been such a blessing. Although in some ways I do stand out, such as the hijab I wear on my head, the head covering, there are still so many ways that I feel so embedded in the fabric that is, you know, our culture. And that's the beautiful thing here, is that it doesn't matter where you come from. There's so many different people from so many different places, of different backgrounds and religions— but here we're all one, one culture. And it's beautiful to see people of, you know, different areas interacting and being family.

Although the conversation between Abu-Salha and Jabeen had not been initially aired, Jabeen got in touch with NPR shortly after the murders and called the station's attention to the interview. The station's local affiliate then broadcast a part of the program, including the paragraph about growing up in America. When President Obama spoke about the murders three days after they occurred, he quoted Abu-Salha directly from the interview.

The walls of Al-Iman are peppered with pictures and references to "Our Three Winners," and every February, the students and teachers there collect food for the hungry in their memory. Jabeen told me that the murders were undoubtedly a hate crime, and who could argue with that? I didn't quite know what to say or ask about the incident when Jabeen told me about it, so I muttered something about how there must be a lot of anger in the community. She agreed that "of course" there's anger, but said that there's also so much more. "Yes, we had to lose our kids," she told me. "We will never be healed. But at least others know who we are as a community, our values. As a school, they are our heroes."

I don't know what someone like Valarie Hodges would say about this story, but I for one think that Louisiana—or any state, for that matter— would be damn lucky to have such a school teaching its children.

* * *

Trying to obtain access to government funds and other types of aid may be a fruitful area for non-Christians to pursue in the future as they continue to demand their rightful place alongside Christians in American public life. The government gives billions of dollars to religion, but not much of it appears to go to minority religious groups or explicitly Atheist organizations.¶¶ Obviously, it is no easy matter for a religious organization or group of religious individuals to start a school or even a nonprofit entity to provide social services to people in need, but it's hardly impossible. When I was researching this chapter, I tried to figure out if any religious tradition had made a focused effort to encourage its churches or believers to pursue government funding. I found very little evidence of any sustained approach. The one real exception involved Hinduism.

In 2005, the Hindu American Foundation, which describes itself on its website as a "non-profit advocacy organization for the Hindu American community," published *Faith-Based and Community Initiatives in the United States: A Guide for Hindu Organizations*. This thirty-six-page document was intended to help Hindu organizations apply for government funding by identifying potential sources of funds, explaining the application process, and describing how to write an effective proposal. It isn't clear whether the guide had any real effects—when I talked to Suhag Shukla, the current executive director of the foundation, she had trouble even locating a copy of the guide and explained that due to "resource disparity" not many Hindu groups have been able to compete for funds—but, at least theoretically, it's a start. What I found particularly interesting about the guide was not the details about where and how to go about applying for money, but rather *why* Hindu organizations ought to apply. In addition to listing the obvious—that these funds would help Hindu organizations provide needed services to people both in the United

---

¶¶ It is important to understand the significant distinction between an institution that is explicitly Atheist and one that is simply neutral regarding religion. The latter takes no position on whether there's a god (or gods or Tao or Heaven or whatever) or not; the former takes the position that there is no god. Many religious people like to claim that public schools promote Atheism, but public schools may not expressly promote Atheism any more than they may expressly promote Christianity or Buddhism or Scientology. Imagine, though, if you will, an expressly Atheist school receiving voucher money. That school would be able to use government funds to explicitly promote the idea that there is no god and that we are all just living temporarily on a big revolving rock spinning around the sun without any real purpose. Just the idea of such a thing makes me want to cry with joy.

States and overseas—the guide also emphasized the role that money can play in helping Hindus become more visible and better understood by the community:

> Hinduism suffers in the United States from misunderstanding and misconceptions. The relative lack of integration of Hindus into the societal mainstream is a likely causative factor—paucity of interaction leads to a paucity of understanding. If explicitly Hindu [faith-based organizations] actively reach out to the community at large and engage in the [faith-based and community initiative] process, Hindus will benefit from increased awareness of their continuing service projects and spread understanding of their pluralistic and tolerant ideals.

In other words—money equals a higher profile equals greater understanding. Perhaps in an ideal world little or no money at all should flow from the government to religion, but that ship has already sailed. The Supreme Court has said that there are very few limits on how the government can funnel funds to religion, and so the question becomes who will apply for the money and who will receive it. If Christian organizations are going to try to get government cash to promote their beliefs, then it only makes sense for non-Christians to do the same.

* * *

The debate about whether the government should provide funding for *private* schools is a contentious one, but probably no issue divides Americans more than what should be done with our *public* schools. After all, most children in the United States attend public schools, and it is in those schools where kids learn many of the values that will shape them for the rest of their lives. What role, if any, should religion play in the public schools? And, specifically, is it okay for Satan to pay those schools a visit? With those crucial questions in mind, we turn to chapter 6.

ATHEISTS, THE ANTICHRIST, AND AFTER-SCHOOL CLUBS

Religious Activities in the Public Schools

LOCATED IN CENTRAL FLORIDA, Orange County encompasses the city of Orlando, and so, in addition to about 1.3 million people, it is also home to both Mickey Mouse and Universal Studios' E.T. In early 2015, however, it almost played host to . . . *SATAN!* The story started in 2011, when a Christian organization named the World Changers of Florida asked the school board if it could distribute Bibles in schools around the county. The board permitted World Changers—whose mission, according to the group's Facebook page, is to "restore personal and national integrity, morals, ethical standards, and direction to the United States as envisioned by our founding fathers in personal correspondence, the Declaration of Independence, the U.S. Constitution, and the Holy Bible"—to place Bibles on a centrally located table for children to take as they pleased during a single day in January 2012. When the group organized a similar passive distribution event the following January, David Williamson and his compatriots at the Central Florida Freethought Community (CFFC) (you may remember them from the chapter on legislative prayer) asked to host a similar event. According to Williamson, "If they're going to have a religious discussion on campus, we need to be a part of it." The board allowed CFFC to make materials such as Thomas Paine's *The Age of Reason* available in about a dozen schools in April of that year, although it also refused to allow CFFC to distribute several other freethinking tracts, such as Sam Harris's *Letter to a Christian Nation* and a book titled *Jesus Is Dead*.

Objecting to what it viewed as censorship of its materials, CFFC sued the school board, but the federal district judge in charge of the case dismissed the suit after the board said that the group could go ahead and distribute any materials it wanted. Due to what seems to be confusion about what it could or could not do, CFFC did not hold another distribution event, but luckily for the citizens of Orange County, the Satanic Temple was there to take CFFC's place. Doug Mesner asked the school board if TST could distribute a little book it had put together, *The Satanic Children's BIG BOOK of Activities*, explaining in a separate statement:

> We would never seek to establish a precedent of disseminating our religious materials in public schools because we believe our constitutional values are better served by respecting a strong separation of Church and State. However, if a public school board is going to allow religious pamphlets and full Bibles to be distributed to students—as is the case in Orange County, Florida—we think the responsible thing to do is to ensure that these students are given access to a variety of differing religious opinions, as opposed to standing idly by while one religious voice dominates the discourse and delivers propaganda to youth.

By this point in the book, you can probably predict what happened next. The community went bonkers, and the board followed suit. The chairman of the board, a guy named Bill Sublette, declared: "This really has, frankly, gotten out of hand. I think we've seen a group or groups take advantage of the open forum we've had." Christine Moore, a fellow board member, announced, "Everyone's upset about the Satanists and the atheists coming." The board quickly halted the religious materials distribution policy, pending review, and then in early 2015 voted 7–1 to prohibit the distribution of any religious materials whatsoever in the public schools. Christians were sad. "This is precisely what the Freedom from Religion people want," said John Stemberger, the head of the Florida Family Policy Council. "They want to get rid of religion, and that's their strategy. And everybody's played into the strategy. It's unfortunate." World Changers vice president Greg Harper compared the ban to the board's earlier decision to ban football chaplains at schools. "They seem to be moving against the interests of a large part of the community," he explained. "The Bible will open somebody's heart, somebody's mind, and cause them to pursue answers." Doug Mesner, on the other hand, thought the change in policy "strongly implie[d] they never intended to have a plurality of voices."

So what exactly is in this scary book of Satanist activities that everyone in Orange County found so alarming? Blood drinking? Child gobbling? Hardly. The book, which sports a full-color cover depicting a smiling girl wearing a pentagram necklace holding hands with a happy boy wearing a shirt with a goat's head on it, is all of eight pages long and doesn't contain a single picture of a sacrificed cat. On the first page, readers are challenged to find six differences between two nearly identical pictures of a girl named Annabel, who is "spreading knowledge and helping to dispel fear and ignorance by demonstrating her Satanic ritual for her class," and her grumpy teacher. The ritual involves a lit candle and a jumping frog, but it's not clear if the teacher is angry about the fire risks posed by the candle or (spoiler alert) the fact that her mug says "I love Homework" in one picture but "#1 Teacher" in the other. Annabel reappears on page three, calling upon readers to color her "study filled with Satanic literature and philosophy" and on page five, a word search in which she and her little friend Damian are using "their patience and open-mindedness to decipher" what Whopper, a "big and sometimes scary" guy who "has trouble saying what's on his mind," is trying to say. The hidden words include such ghastly Satanic epithets as "friends," "love," and "acceptance."

Damian, for his part, also appears on page four, where he uses a connect-the-dots picture to show his classmates (and the grumpy teacher) how to "make an inverted pentagram," and then again on page six, a maze, in which he and his pet dog, Cerberus, "are trying to navigate [a] dark, dank labyrinth to find the fabled Necronomicon." Completing the book are pages on which children can draw a picture of what Cerberus might be dreaming about, decode the secret message that Annabel sent Damian in a note during class (the teacher looks really pissed off about this particular infraction; the ruler she brandishes in her hand is probably symbolic of the corporal punishment that TST has vocally opposed), and unjumble mixed-up letters to spell more devilish terms like "compassion," "respect," and "empathy." This latter puzzle is accompanied by a picture of three mean bullies threatening a waving Damian and his bespectacled friend and says, by way of direction: "These bullies are mad and afraid of things they don't understand. Help Damian use inclusive language to defuse the situation."

I don't know about you, but I sure sleep a lot better knowing that the Orange County school board kept this dissolute tract away from impressionable schoolchildren!

* * *

Given that the great majority of children in the United States attend public schools, it should be no surprise that those schools have long been a major battleground in the church/state wars. School-age kids, particularly those in elementary schools, are highly susceptible to being influenced by adult authority figures, so it would make sense that Christians seeking to bolster their religious communities would try to get as big a foothold in the public schools as possible. This is still the case today. As journalist Katherine Stewart writes in her masterful 2012 book *The Good News Club: The Christian Right's Stealth Assault on America's Children*: "It is now accepted wisdom [among many of the modern missionary groups] that the most fruitful targets of conversion efforts are children between the ages of four and fourteen. . . . Schools are especially attractive because small children are easily swayed by representatives of authority, such as teachers and school officials."

Fortunately, the Supreme Court, in contrast to its rulings in other areas of Establishment Clause law, has done a fairly decent job in keeping state-supported religion out of the public schools. Although students are rightly free to pray voluntarily at school, either by themselves or together in groups, for example, the Court has placed strict limits on school-sponsored prayer, meaning any prayer that is organized or led by teachers, administrators, or other government employees who work at the school. In two of the most unpopular cases ever decided by the Court—*Engel v. Vitale* from 1962 and *Abington School District v. Schempp* from 1963—the Court invalidated school-sponsored prayers and Bible readings on the grounds that, among other things, they coerce nonbelievers into participation. As the Court explained in *Engel*, "When the power, prestige and financial support of government is placed behind a particular religious belief, the indirect coercive pressure upon religious minorities to conform to the prevailing officially approved religion is plain." Several decades later, the Court followed up these decisions by striking down school-organized prayers at graduation ceremonies and football games. The majorities in these deeply divided cases felt that the same "subtle coercive pressure" that exists within the classroom can be experienced in other school contexts. In the graduation case of *Lee v. Weisman* from 1992, for instance, Justice Kennedy's majority opinion cited "research in psychology" for the proposition that "adolescents are often susceptible to pressure from their peers towards conformity" and observed, "What to most believers may seem nothing more than a reasonable request that the nonbeliever respect their religious practices, in a school context may appear to the nonbeliever or dissenter to be an attempt to employ the machinery of the State to enforce a religious orthodoxy."

On other issues arising within the public schools, the Court has also appropriately policed the line between acceptable and unconstitutional church-state interactions. For instance, in a case mentioned in chapter 1, *Stone v. Graham*, from 1980, the Court invalidated a Kentucky law that required all public schools to post copies of the Ten Commandments in every classroom. And in two cases—*Epperson v. Arkansas* from 1968 and *Edwards v. Aguillard* from 1987—the Court struck down state efforts to interfere with how public schools taught the "theory" of evolution. The *Epperson* case involved a statute much like the one at issue in the famous *Scopes* trial, which prohibited schools from teaching evolution altogether, while *Edwards* was about a Louisiana statute that required schools that taught evolution to spend equal time teaching "creation science." In both cases, the Court found that the statutes lacked any plausible secular purpose; in *Edwards*, for example, the Court rightly dismissed the state's purported purpose in promoting "academic freedom" as "a sham."

When it comes to how public schools can manage their classrooms after school hours, however, the Court's decisions have been a bit more questionable. In a line of cases, the Court has pretty much said that if a public school opens its classrooms up for use by social or recreational groups outside of official school hours, then it must allow religious groups to use those classrooms also, even if those groups are worshipping or even proselytizing elementary school–age children. To understand these cases, we have to go back to the public forum doctrine that I talked about in chapters 2 and 3. Public schools do not have to make their facilities available for use by recreational and social groups, so if they choose to do so, they essentially create a designated limited public forum for speech. Remember from chapter 2 that the Court's basic free speech rule regarding designated limited public forums is that the government can restrict speech within the forum on the basis of the subject matter of that speech but generally cannot restrict speech on the basis of its viewpoint—a position that naturally raises the question of whether religion is a subject matter or a viewpoint. Moreover, even if religion is a viewpoint and therefore generally cannot be excluded from the forum, can a public school nonetheless defend its decision to exclude religion on the basis that the exclusion is necessary to avoid violating the Establishment Clause's prohibition on promoting or endorsing religion?

The first of these cases, *Widmar v. Vincent* from 1981, actually involved a public university rather than an elementary or secondary school. When the University of Missouri at Kansas City—which allowed more than a hundred student groups to use its facilities when they were not being used for academic purposes—barred a religious group from using those same facilities, students in the religious group sued, claiming that the policy violated its free speech rights. A lower court held that the university's policy was not only acceptable but also actually required under the Establishment Clause, because if the school had allowed religious groups to use its facilities, it would have been "giving prohibited support to an institution of religion." The Supreme Court disagreed, finding that the exclusion of religious groups amounted to viewpoint-based discrimination that could be justified only if including those groups would have unconstitutionally promoted religion. On the latter issue, the Court concluded that any benefit accruing to religion from letting religious groups participate alongside nonreligious groups was "merely incidental" and thus not unconstitutional. It was important to the Court that the forum would be "available to a broad class of nonreligious as well as religious speakers" and that including religion in the forum would not "confer any imprimatur of state approval of religious sects or practices."

A dozen years later, in 1993, the Court extended this analysis to public elementary and secondary schools in *Lamb's Chapel v. Center Moriches Union Free School District*. In that case, the New York state school district had opened school property to social, civic, recreational, and political organizations during non-school hours but had specifically prohibited the use of school premises by "any group for religious purposes." An evangelical church asked the district if it could use school property to show a six-part film series titled *Turn Your Heart toward Home*, which addressed various family-related issues, including child-rearing, from a Christian perspective. When the district refused, the church sued, and the Supreme Court ruled unanimously in the church's favor. The Court observed that the school district was free to make subject-matter distinctions but not viewpoint ones when deciding how broadly to extend its designated limited public forum, and so it framed the "critical question" as "whether it discriminates on the basis of viewpoint to permit school property to be used for the presentation of all views about family issues and child rearing except those dealing with the subject matter from a religious viewpoint." Framed that way, the question was easy to answer—the school district could have prohibited any organization from meeting to discuss family issues and child-rearing, but having opened the forum up to that subject, it could not then exclude religious perspectives on the subject from the forum.

The *Widmar* and *Lamb's Chapel* cases set the stage for the much more difficult case of *Good News Club v. Milford Central School*, which was decided in 2000. Good News Club is a creation of the Child Evangelism Fellowship (CEF), a group whose stated purpose, according to its website, is "to evangelize boys and girls with the Gospel of the Lord Jesus Christ and to establish (disciple) them in the Word of God and in a local church for Christian living." Founded in 1937, with its headquarters in Warrenton, Missouri, CEF is a gigantic organization, with 700 full-time workers and 40,000 volunteers. According to the group's statement of faith, its members believe that the Bible "is inerrant in the original writing and that its teaching and authority are absolute, supreme and final" and that "the souls of those who have trusted the Lord Jesus Christ for salvation do at death immediately pass into His presence."* To save the children, CEF runs Good News Clubs in public schools throughout the country. At the meetings, which ordinarily and purposefully begin as soon after the end of the school day as possible, the group's volunteer leader teaches the children (who attend only with the permission of their parents) a lesson from the Bible. The lessons are not dry and boring like the ones I remember from my own Hebrew School days, but are rather fun affairs, or, as CEF's website puts it, "an action-packed time," complete with games and songs. And treats. Don't forget the treats! As the particular club involved in the case that went to the Supreme Court described its own activities to the attorney of the town of Milford, New York:

> The Club opens its session with Ms. Fournier taking attendance. As she calls a child's name, if the child recites a Bible verse the child receives a treat. After attendance, the Club sings songs. Next Club members engage in games that involve, *inter alia*, learning Bible verses. Ms. Fournier then relates a Bible story and explains how it applies to Club members' lives. The Club closes with prayer. Finally, Ms. Fournier distributes treats and the Bible verses for memorization.

The case arose when, in 1996, the aforementioned Ms. Fournier and her husband asked the Milford School District if they could use the school's cafeteria for meetings of the Good News Club. The town's policy allowed groups to use school facilities after school hours for "instruction in any branch of education, learning or the arts" or for "social, civic and recreational meetings and entertainment events, and other uses pertaining to the welfare of the community." Applying this policy, the town rejected the club's request on the grounds that as "religious instruction and Bible

---

* On the flip side, however, those souls who do not trust the Lord Jesus Christ for salvation will "remain after death in misery until the final judgment of the great white throne, when soul and body reunited at the resurrection shall be cast 'Into the lake of fire' which is 'the second death,' to be 'punished with everlasting destruction from the presence of the Lord, and from the glory of His power'" (internal quotations, designated by single quotes, are from various scary biblical passages).

study," the purpose of the club fell outside the approved uses. The club sued and lost in the lower courts—according to the Second Circuit Court of Appeals, the subject matter of the club's activities was "quintessentially religious," and thus excluding it from the limited public forum established by the town was "constitutional subject matter discrimination, not unconstitutional viewpoint discrimination."

The club appealed to the Supreme Court, which, in a majority opinion written by Justice Thomas, ruled in favor of the club. For Thomas and the justices who joined him, the case was basically indistinguishable from *Lamb's Chapel*. As Thomas explained, the "only apparent difference" between the two cases was that the club taught its moral lessons "through live storytelling and prayer, whereas Lamb's Chapel taught lessons through films," a distinction that Thomas described as "inconsequential," since "both modes of speech use a religious viewpoint." As in the earlier case of *Lamb's Chapel*, here the Town of Milford had excluded the club simply because it approached the subject matter of morals and character from a religious perspective. "[S]peech discussing otherwise permissible subjects cannot be excluded from a limited public forum on the ground that the subject is discussed from a religious viewpoint," Thomas wrote. "Thus, we conclude that Milford's exclusion of the Club from use of the school . . . constitutes impermissible viewpoint discrimination."

The dissenting justices, particularly Justice Stevens and Justice Souter, thought the case was about as similar to *Lamb's Chapel* as it was to a lamb chop. Justice Souter, for instance, wrote that the facts "differ from those in *Lamb's Chapel* as night from day" because the Good News Club was holding "an evangelical service of worship calling children to commit themselves in an act of Christian conversion" rather than simply discussing "a subject from a particular, Christian point of view." Justice Stevens broke it down even more carefully. He suggested that there are really three categories of religious speech: (1) speech about a topic from a religious point of view; (2) religious speech intended to proselytize or inculcate belief in others; and (3) worship. According to Stevens, only the first type of speech is protected in this context. Analogizing to political clubs, Stevens said that just like Milford doesn't have to "allow organized political groups" like the Democratic Party "to hold meetings, the principal purpose of which is . . .

to recruit others to join their respective groups," so too could it exclude religious groups trying to do the same thing. "[D]istinguishing speech from a religious viewpoint on the one hand, from religious proselytizing on the other," Stevens wrote, "is comparable to distinguishing meetings to discuss political issues from meetings whose principal purpose is to recruit new members to join a political organization." Both political recruitment and religious proselytizing groups, Stevens theorized, might be excluded, since they could "introduce divisiveness and tend to separate young children into cliques that undermine the school's educational mission."

The justices were divided as well on the Establishment Clause question. The dissenters thought that a school that allowed the club to operate on its premises might indeed risk violating the Establishment Clause, although these justices would have sent the case back to the lower courts to do more fact-finding on the issue. For example, Justice Souter thought that "the timing and format of Good News's gatherings may well affirmatively suggest the imprimatur of officialdom in the minds of the young children," since "the club is open solely to elementary students, only four outside groups have been identified as meeting in the school, and Good News is, seemingly, the only one whose instruction follows immediately on the conclusion of the official schoolday." Justice Thomas was not persuaded. "We decline to employ Establishment Clause jurisprudence using a modified heckler's veto," he wrote, "in which a group's activity can be proscribed on the basis of what the youngest members of the audience might misperceive."

* * *

In the wake of the Court's decision in *Good News Club*, the number of Good News Clubs actually operating in the country's public schools skyrocketed. As reported by Katherine Stewart, who wrote an entire book about these clubs (and related Christian activities in the public schools), 3,500 clubs had sprung up in schools across the nation by 2009. In fact, the extent of the clubs' growth practically became a mantra at the CEF's 2010 national convention, held at the Shocco Springs Baptist Conference Center in Talladega, Alabama. According to the left-leaning Stewart, who attended the conference incognito (wearing a "knee-length skirt" and with her hair "pulled back in a prim braid" to fit in with the crowd), the figure "728 percent" came up again and again during the speeches and presentations she sat through, representing the increase in the number of kids participating in the clubs.

Stewart's research also suggests that Good News Clubs are actively trying both to make students think that the clubs are part of the schools where they operate and to get their member students to bring in non-members. On the former point, Stewart's investigation of the Good News Club operating at an elementary school in the Loyal Heights neighborhood in Seattle concludes that "there was ample evidence that the leaders of the Good News Club efforts were aware that they might be perceived as a school-sponsored group—and were pleased about it. Indeed it is certain that their very purpose in being in the school was to be perceived as part of the school." On the recruitment of non-members, she observes, "It takes only a little experience with the CEF to understand that its primary intended target is not just the children whose parents sign them up, but also the children of parents who do not volunteer for their children to participate." Regarding this observation, Stewart quotes both a parent of a non-member from Loyal Heights who told her that the kids in the club are informed that they'll get "candy and prizes" if they recruit friends to the club, and a CEF leader from Santa Barbara, who told Stewart "with a smirk and a shrug of feigned helplessness," that "we are not allowed to approach the children who aren't in the club. . . . But we can't stop the children from approaching other children." And the clubs are hardly tolerant of those who do not share their preferred faith. After reading through CEF's printed materials, Stewart reports:

In the fine lawyering supplied by the CEF's well-funded defenders, the Good News Club is characterized as a form of "moral instruction" from a "religious viewpoint." It is that, too, but that is hardly the whole truth. The CEF teaches not just morals, but also religious doctrines. In the CEF's own literature, public schools are "mission fields," and evangelizing in public schools is characterized as "harvest work." Children of other faiths are "unreached" and need to be "counseled for Salvation". . . . Children who attend the clubs are emphatically told that "nonbelievers" are going to hell, to be "separated from God forever."

The *Good News* case not only opened the doors of public school class-rooms to evangelizing Christian groups, but also helped embolden Christians seeking to distribute religious literature and other materials—outside of school hours, anyway—to public school students. After all, if a school allows private groups to send home flyers with students or to distribute information to students—say in the hallway after classes are over—then it most likely, under the logic of *Good News Club* and other similar cases,† must allow religious groups to distribute their information on an equal basis. Consequently, as Stewart concludes, "many public schools today are awash in religious literature." She expounds:

> The Gideons International, the Bible-distributing ministry, passes out tens of thousands of Bibles each year at public schools and, through its Life Book Movement initiative, has distributed more than half a million evangelical Christian religious tracts, written with teenagers in mind, on public school campuses. LivingWaters, a California-based ministry, targets public high school students with a special edition of Darwin's classic book, *On the Origin of Species*, that includes a creationist introduction. In Montgomery County, Maryland, a Christian group was allowed to distribute flyers touting "ex gay conversion therapy" to students in the county's schools in 2010. And flyers advertising Good News Clubs go home in children's backpacks all over the country.

Okay, so the public schools are filled with Christian literature and Christian after-school groups. No shock there, given the Court's decisions in this area. But what happens when a non-Christian group tries to distribute its materials to students or tries to set up its own after-school club?

---

† Particularly relevant here is the Court's 1995 decision in Rosenberger v. Rector and Visitors of University of Virginia, which held that a public university could not exclude a religious publication from a general funding program authorizing the payment of outside firms for printing student publications. This case probably deserves more attention here than I'm giving it in this footnote, but it's really complicated, and the Good News Club case makes the point more clearly and succinctly.

* * *

It may come as a surprise that attempts by Atheists and Satanists to distribute their materials in the public schools have not always ended in complete chaos. A seemingly rare success story on this score comes from Delta County in western Colorado. In December 2015, after the school district allowed the Gideons to hand out free Bibles to students, a concerned mother and member of the Western Colorado Atheists and Freethinkers contacted FFRF, which then asked the school for permission to distribute Atheist materials. Although the request was certainly controversial (the president of the Colorado Freethinkers group claimed that its members received death threats over the incident), the district allowed the giveaway, issuing a statement explaining that because the district had an open distribution policy, and because the proposed literature did not violate that policy's restrictions on hate speech, political speech, commercial advertisement, or obscenity, the district had to allow FFRF to circulate its Atheist literature. According to an AP story about the issue, the district spokesperson even expressed his view that "students would not be hurt by the giveaway and might also learn about different views on religion." A local pastor publicly supported the district's decision, telling a news reporter, "We want our kids to be able to access different types of materials, for example 4-H, and Boy Scouts, Girl Scouts. Once we do that, we cannot discriminate against any other groups being able to distribute that material."

On April 1, 2016, a date apparently chosen because it was the day when the county's standardized testing ended,‡ the school allowed FFRF to place copies of pamphlets like *It's Okay to Not Believe in God!* and *What Is a Freethinker?* and one about sex in the Bible (that the district kind of censored with some strategically placed stickers), on a public distribution table. The Satanic Temple also sent along some copies of *The Satanic Children's BIG BOOK of Activities* for good measure. According to the AP account, some of the materials were completely gone by the middle of the day, although the story did not mention whether they were taken by

---

‡   Hmmmm. Seems fishy

students curious about Atheism or by Christians who wanted to throw them into a fire. In the wake of the giveaway, there was some talk about the district possibly amending its distribution policy, but it's not clear whether it actually went through with that idea.

Other efforts to distribute non-Christian literature in the public schools have not gone so well. The controversy in Orange County, Florida, with which this chapter opened, is the most prominent example, but not the only one. Stewart, for instance, reports an incident from the town of Miami, Oklahoma, where a school that had allowed a Bible distribution refused to allow a family of Muslims to give out copies of the Qur'an. According to Stewart, "The family received so much hate mail that they feared for their lives."

Another incident that Stewart covered involved the school district in Albemarle County, Virginia. In 2006, in a case brought by none other than the Child Evangelism Fellowship, the Fourth Circuit Court of Appeals, whose law governs Virginia, held that public school districts that allow private groups to send flyers home to parents through a school-facilitated "take-home flyer policy" could not exclude CEF from sending flyers about its Good News Club; citing the Supreme Court's decision in *Good News Club* repeatedly, the court suggested that such an exclusion would amount to unconstitutional viewpoint discrimination.

Following that case, a Unitarian Universalist Church asked the Albemarle County school district to distribute a flyer inviting "children of all ages" to "explore the traditions of December and their origins, followed by a Pagan ritual to celebrate Yule." The flyer had images of a cross, a Jewish star, and a pentagram printed on it. Some local Christians were not happy. One blogger complained that the flyer should not have been sent home, noting that a "pagan ritual" was "an educational experience my children don't need." A pastor from Charlottesville used the incident as evidence that Christians should take their kids out of the public schools. A year later, things got even more heated when a camp for "Atheists, Freethinkers, Humanists, Brights, or whatever" asked the same school district to send home its brochures. This time, some of the teachers actually refused to include Camp Quest's flyer in their take-home packets. According to a representative of the teachers, many teachers were "disgusted" with the flyer; in fact, the anonymous representative him- or herself told a reporter that the flyer "was pretty offensive and pretty outrageous." Stewart reported that the school district subsequently "cancel[ed] the backpack flyer program altogether."

Discord has also occasionally popped up when non-Christian groups have tried to start after-school clubs alongside the Good News Clubs. Students seeking to form Atheist clubs, for instance, have run into trouble, according to a 2012 article in the *Washington Post*, which reported about a school in Melbourne, Florida, that rejected an Atheist club more than once for being "too controversial."

Perhaps the most publicized example of such an incident comes from Pisgah High School in North Carolina, where in 2014 Ben Wilson, a student who tried to start an Atheist group at the school, was told to join a different club instead because his wouldn't "be successful considering the school's makeup." When Ben left the school halfway through the year, his fifteen-year-old sister, Kalei, tried once again to start such a club but was also rebuffed. In response, FFRF and the North Carolina ACLU chapter sent a letter to the school reminding it of the law. The letter had the desired effect, and the school agreed to let Kalei start the club. Nearly a dozen students showed interest in joining, and two teachers agreed to sponsor it, but Kalei ultimately decided not to follow through on her plan after receiving what Americans United referred to as a "torrent" of threats and verbal attacks from members of the community. More recently, in late 2017, when Elijah Gregg, a Pagan father in Demorest, Georgia, saw the Good News Club flyer that his kindergartener brought home from school, he asked the board of education in the town how he could start a Pagan group for students. He got no real answer from the board, but he did receive a visit at home from a Boy Scouts volunteer, who told him that the school district would "shut down all after-school activities" before it would allow Gregg to form a Pagan club.

Encouragingly, both Muslims and Atheists have created national organizations intended, at least in part, to help high school students form groups at their local schools. The Muslim Interscholastic Tournament (MIST) was formed in Houston in 2002 to bring Muslim high school students together at tournaments around the country for competitions in

activities like public speaking. According to its website, MIST is "dedicated to empowering high school students by giving them a venue to,"
among other things, "learn strategies to deal with stereotypes and prejudices against Islam and Muslims." MIST's website has a page devoted
to helping Muslim secondary school students start their own "Muslim
Student Associations" to "educate people" about Islam and to "correct
stereotypes." The site has a lot of practical advice for students, including
the need for persistence: "You may experience some reluctance from the
faculty and the administration when starting your MSA. That's why your
core group should be persistent. They shouldn't quit after the first bump
in the road. If you come up against any reluctance, emphasize that your
MSA is for anyone interested in learning and clearing up misconceptions
about Islam. This may facilitate school approval." The site reiterates the
need for education about Islam, providing advice to students about how
to find a sponsor willing to direct the group:

> Remind the sponsor that teachers are, above all, educators who believe
> in the institution of education. In this post 9/11 climate, intolerance and
> aggression are bred from ignorance. As an educator, it is important to
> sustain a welcoming environment to promote education, prevent intoler-
> ance, clear stereotypes, and lessen aggression due to misunderstanding. . . .
> Your MSA's purpose is to provide leadership and education to both its
> members and the community. Tell your teacher that by sponsoring the
> MSA, he/she is creating an environment for Muslims to learn about their
> religion and for people of other faiths to become educated about Islam.
> Stress the point that education on Islam is needed by both Muslims and
> non-Muslims to help ease intolerance and unite people.

The Secular Student Alliance (SSA) serves a similar function for secular
students. Founded in 2000, the SSA defines its purpose as empowering
"secular students to proudly express their identity, build welcoming communities, promote secular values, and set a course for lifelong activism."
Although the organization is aimed primarily at college students, it has
also invested significant resources toward helping secular students at the
high school level. A page on its website is devoted to high school students,

declaring at the outset: "As a secular student in a high school, it can be a challenging experience to make a go on your own. Don't worry though! We are here to help connect you with like-minded students both in your own local school and community, as well as across the nation." The rest of the page offers links to help students who need legal advice ("We're here to help if you are having any kind of legal trouble at your school regarding the separation of church and state or the rights of non-theists. Let us know!"), want to get involved in service projects, would like to connect online with other secular-minded students, or are interested in starting "secular safe zones" or affiliate SSA groups at their local schools. According to the website, there are more than two hundred affiliate SSA groups at colleges and high schools around the country, twenty-eight of which are at high schools, some located in perhaps surprising, not particularly secular states like Alabama, North Carolina, and Texas.

To learn more about the SSA, I headed to Columbus, Ohio, in July 2016 to attend the organization's fifteenth annual national conference, at Ohio State University. It was quite a scene. More than two hundred secular students showed up to meet like-minded people, listen to inspirational secular speakers, and attend panel discussions about different aspects of forming secular clubs and communities at their local schools. I'm not sure I had ever previously seen anything I would have described as embodying "secular spirit," but that's the best phrase to characterize what people seemed to be feeling during the conference.

The executive assistant of SSA kicked things off at an "opening ceremony," where she jumped excitedly around like a cruise director welcoming passengers onto the *Pacific Princess*,§ asked the audience if we were "pumped for fun," ran a cringe-worthy "Quiz Game" about conference rules ("True or False: You should throw all your trash on the ground?"), and explained that attendees wearing red lanyards (as opposed to the regular ones) were not yet "out" as Atheists and did not want to appear in photos or videos posted on social media sites. The average age of those at the conference was roughly twenty, and the entire event had the stamp

---

§   At one point she said, "We try to do more than yell Atheism, Atheism, ya ya ya, but we do that too."

of the Millennials upon it. The conference guidebook, for instance, had an entire page dedicated to anti-harassment policies ("Please ask which pronouns a person prefers; respect and call people what they ask you to call them.") and another containing rules about "form[ing] a physical relationship with a fellow attendee," including a reminder that the age of consent in Ohio is sixteen. I've been to many, many conferences in my day, but this was the first one where the tote bag included a condom amid the typical stickers, pens, and promotional materials. Even with the condom, though, I decided to skip the eight-thirty p.m. session titled "Getting It On at the Con: How to Get Lucky Consensually."

If I had to identify an overarching theme for the conference, it would be that Humanists and other secularists should go out into the world and actively serve their communities to (among other things) spread the idea that one does not need to believe in god to be good. Speaker after speaker echoed this theme. For instance, in his opening talk, Fernando Alcántar, a former religious youth leader turned self-described "gaytheist," urged his fellow Humanists to "wake up and act." He told the audience that Atheists and Humanists cannot just be "busy reading papers and making discoveries," leaving the business of saving people to churches and religion. Atheists must change their image, he urged, so they are not viewed as "just geeks and angry people." Other speakers spoke about "taking secular activism off campus" and using secularism "to shape a more just world." Still another panelist told the attendees that "secularism does not exist in a bubble" and pressed everyone to "take action on your values."

Although many of the panels and speeches addressed various aspects of secularism generally, others were directly aimed at helping students form successful clubs back at their home institutions. The conference ran workshops on topics like group leadership, fund-raising, and using social media. I was particularly interested in a couple of panels that focused on how secular student groups should work together with other types of groups, including religious ones, on campus. At a panel titled "Coalition Building—Why It's So Important," a speaker urged students to support other campus groups and to try and find common ground with them, even if it "involves snacks." This speaker told the audience that "it's good to have Christian groups having your back" and that secular groups "gotta stand with those Wiccans." "They need to be out more," he continued, speaking of the Wiccans, "so we can know what they do."

Although there was certainly a good amount of anti-religion rhetoric bopping around at the conference, I was heartened by the session titled "Interfaith Engagement Is Important!" facilitated by Nicole Niebler, president of the University of Wisconsin Atheists, Humanists, and Agnostics. Niebler told her secular audience not to assume "that you know what all religious people believe," explaining that "the young generation of believers is more open than our parents' generation." Speaking of religious campus organizations, she said that although "you don't have to go pray with them . . . if they have a social event, go," and told the people in the room to try and defy Atheist stereotypes: "Don't argue about everything. Don't show frustration if they say 'bless you.' Be nice," she urged, although she did concede that "if they're trying to get demons out of you, you should probably leave." Joking aside, though, Niebler persuasively suggested to her audience that true interfaith engagement means "actually being open-minded" and being willing to respect the opinions of people with whom we disagree.

Hey, maybe a healthy religiously pluralistic public square is possible after all!

* * *

Last, but hardly least, there's the Satanic Temple's "After School Satan" (ASS) initiative. TST launched ASS in the fall of 2016 to counter the presence of Good News Clubs in the public schools. The idea was to start ASS clubs in schools around the country that already had Good News Clubs operating in them; in fact, TST's official policy has always been to sponsor ASS clubs *only* in those schools. Although the official launch video of the initiative is super-creepy and features lots of spiders, the content of TST's clubs is actually even more innocuous than *The Satanic Children's BIG BOOK of Activities*, which caused such a brouhaha in Orange County, Florida. For one thing, the clubs are only vaguely related to Satanism. According to the permission slip that TST sends to parents who might want to sign their kids up for the ASS clubs, "After School Satan is an exciting, fun-filled hour once a month" that offers science, creative learning activities, songs, art projects, and educational stories to teach children skills and values such as "basic critical reasoning," "problem solving," and "creative expression." According to the ASS website's FAQs:

> All *After School Satan Clubs* are based upon a uniform syllabus that emphasizes a scientific, rationalist, non-superstitious world view. While the twisted Evangelical teachings of the *Good News Clubs* "robs children of the innocence and enjoyment of childhood, replacing them with a negative self image, preoccupation with sin, fear of Hell, and aversion to critical thinking," *After School Satan Clubs* incorporate games, projects, and thinking exercises that help children understand how we know what we know about our world and our universe.

TST's original idea was that TST members would run the clubs, which meant that the clubs would have to be located near local chapters. During the 2016–17 school year, TST was able to get a few clubs up and running, including a couple in the Pacific Northwest. Of course, the ASS clubs were not generally greeted by communities with open arms. According to an official from America Needs Fatima, the same group that organized the anti-Satanist rally in Belle Plaine, Minnesota, more than 87,000 people signed a petition against the clubs, urging schools, in this official's words, "NOT to allow Satan—the father of lies—into the lives of young children." When the city of Tacoma, Washington, approved an ASS club to meet at the Point Defiance Elementary School, parents asked the school board to reverse its decision, but to no avail. When the club held its first open house at the school for both parents and students, Catholics gathered nearby to pray the rosary "for the protection of our kids in the community," according to a local reverend, who also claimed that his flock was praying for the souls of TST members. Yet another representative of America Needs Fatima added that TST "attacks God, undermines moral values and foments disrespect for legitimate authority." About twenty people—half adults, half kids—attended the open house, and according to Lilith Starr, the head of TST's Seattle chapter, the event was a success.

In the fall of 2017, TST changed its policy to allow volunteers not necessarily affiliated with TST to run its ASS groups, with the hope that this strategy would result in more clubs being started around the country. When I wrote this in June 2018, it was not clear whether this tactic was working or what the future of the ASS initiative would be. The club in Tacoma folded for lack of interest (only one student showed up), and although the "Find a Club" page on the ASS website at one point listed eighteen schools and school districts where TST "offered to present [its] curriculum," the page did not state whether any of those districts was in fact hosting a club.

TST clearly had a number of objectives in mind when it decided to launch the ASS project, but I think one in particular is worth emphasizing—namely, that by participating in public life through these clubs, the organization hoped to educate nonbelievers about the nature of Satanism and the qualities of the people who believe in it. As Doug Mesner told *People* magazine shortly after the initiative was launched, "Our goal is that when people see things from our perspective, they'll look beyond the stereotypical assumptions about our group. It really is possible to identify as a Satanist and live a moral, productive life." As I will argue in the concluding chapter, this type of education is one of the best justifications for minorities to step up and demand their rightful place next to Christians in American public life.

CONCLUSION

IN KEEPING WITH the rhetorician's old saw, "Tell them what you're going to tell them; then tell them; then tell them what you told them," I will begin this last chapter with a brief summary of the four key points that I've tried to show so far in the book.

First, I've suggested that in a series of cases going back roughly two or three decades, the Supreme Court has made it clear that the government may, consistent with the Establishment Clause of the First Amendment, open up public property, institutions, and funds to religious individuals and groups, so long as it treats all religious viewpoints the same. In *Capitol Square Review and Advisory Board v. Pinette*, the Court held that privately sponsored religious symbols displayed in a public forum created by the government will almost certainly survive a First Amendment challenge, even if some people might be confused about whether the symbols are endorsed by the government. In *Town of Greece v. Galloway*, the Court held that local government bodies like town boards can begin their proceedings with openly sectarian prayers, even if those invocations may deeply offend nonbelievers or even coerce them into participating in the prayer. In *Zelman v. Simmons-Harris*, the Court held that a school voucher program funded with government money can include private religious schools, even if those religious schools end up receiving nearly all of the money. And in *Good News Club v. Milford Central School*, the Court held that if a public school opens up its facilities to after-school groups, it must let religious groups use the facilities, even if those groups are employing games and treats to proselytize and inculcate elementary school children in the faith.

Second, although I haven't always lingered on what seems to be a fairly obvious point, I've suggested that Christians have taken advantage of these cases to participate widely in American public life. Voucher programs are filled with Christian schools, which receive the vast majority of the money distributed by those programs. Public spaces are speckled with Christian displays and monuments. Public schools are jam-packed with Good News Clubs that are proselytizing extremely young kids with the so-called truth of Christianity. And legislatures and local government bodies across the country regularly open their proceedings with Christian prayers that explicitly refer to God and Jesus Christ.

Third, I've documented how in the wake of the Court's recent decisions, non-Christians—including both Atheists and members of minority religious groups—have begun to demand their place in American public life. Groups like the Summum, the American Atheists, and the Satanic Temple have asked to have their monuments erected on government property. Various Atheist groups, Wiccans, and others have put up temporary religious displays alongside crèches and other Christian holiday symbols in public parks and buildings. Hindus, Wiccans, and Atheists have given prayers and invocations before legislatures and town boards. Muslims have used public voucher money to fund their private schools, while Scientologists and others have used public money to fund their social service programs and projects. Secularists and Satanists have started their own after-school clubs in the classrooms of public schools across the nation. It is impossible to calculate exactly how much of this type of participation has occurred, but it appears that the phenomenon has increased over time and is starting to become at least somewhat widespread.

Fourth, and finally, I've explained how majority Christian communities* have often met these requests by minorities to participate in public life with ignorance, anger, hostility, and even hatred. This kind of reaction has not been universal—think, for example, about the Town of Greece's polite reception of Linda Stephens's secular invocation—but it has been distressingly common. Atheist holiday displays have been vandalized. Invocations offered by Muslims, Hindus, and others have been canceled, interrupted, and insulted. After-school programs run by secularists and Satanists have been opposed for no reason other than prejudice. Often the opposition has come from members of the public, but government officials have hardly been friendly to those in the minority. For years, the federal government resisted allowing Wiccans to have pentacles placed on the gravestones of loved ones because the president of the United States, among other high-level officials, didn't like witches. State legislators have opposed allowing Muslim schools to participate in voucher programs that funnel enormous amounts of money to Christian schools. Town leaders have turned their backs on courageous non-Christians who have dared to pray before their boards. Local officials have insulted and defamed members of the Satanic Temple with scant understanding of what the group believes or does.

I wrote this book primarily to make the four points just reiterated; accordingly, most of its pages have been devoted to that project. I also, however, want to explain why I believe that the relatively new phenomenon of non-Christians' demanding their rightful place in American public life is something that should be applauded, celebrated, and continued.

---

* For the sake of clarity, I would like to reiterate what I said in the introduction about how Christians are not all the same: *Christians are not all the same.* It may seem that by invoking "Christians" and "Christian communities" and the like, I'm suggesting some sort of uniform negative Christian response to minority demands for participation in public life. I am not. Just because many communities have reacted to minority participation in public life with hostility draped in Christianity does not mean that all Christians oppose such participation; indeed, many may welcome it, although if they do, their voices tend not to be nearly as loud as those of the objectors.

* * *

Let me start by appealing to those readers who believe that the only acceptable public square is a completely (or at least mostly) secular one. The view that public life should be free of religion is a position that holds great force in a society where everyone is entitled to be treated equally and the government is supposed to represent all of its constituents. From the perspective of minorities, the widespread participation of Christianity in American public life—as I've used that phrase throughout this book—poses a number of serious dangers. For one thing, the entanglement of Christianity and government threatens to coerce minorities, in both explicit and subtle ways, to act in concert with the religious majority. Think, for example, of the Jewish citizen who comes to a town board to ask for a zoning ordinance and feels that she has to stand up for the board's Christian prayer to get a fair shake, or the Atheist parent who fears that his seven-year-old child is going to want to join her public school's Good News Club to fit in and get treats.

Beyond coercion, when the government gives large amounts of money to Christians or erects Christian symbols on its property or starts a legislative meeting with a prayer to Jesus, the action inevitably results in minorities feeling excluded, offended, and injured. Justice O'Connor had it exactly right when she suggested that government endorsement of religion causes nonbelievers to feel like lesser members of society and the political community. And then, of course, there's always the possibility that Christian beliefs will directly influence the development and execution of public policy to the detriment of minorities and that providing support for the majority religion will give Christianity a further advantage in the marketplace for followers, which at least for some minorities may be a significant concern.

As it turns out, though, demanding minority participation in public life is likely, however counterintuitively, to be the best hope for creating a secular public square in the United States. Over the course of writing this book, I've related numerous stories of Christian majorities' closing down a public forum rather than allowing minorities to take part alongside Christians, thus voluntarily creating a secular public square even though the Supreme Court has said that such a square is not constitutionally required. Think, for example, of the Phoenix City Council canceling its invocation policy to keep Satan out of town, or Orange County, Florida, changing its policy to prohibit distribution of religious literature so that children there wouldn't be exposed to dangerous word search puzzles, or the town of Belle Plaine getting rid of its public forum for private religious speech rather than allowing there to be two monuments honoring veterans instead of one.

Part of me is tempted to end the book right here, since any course of action that has some chance of creating a secular public square is an improvement over the current alternative. I will resist the urge, though, because it's important to explain why, even if the Christian majority decides not to close down a public forum in response to minority demands for equal participation, the religiously cacophonous public square that could result is similarly more desirable than the current alternative.

Before we go any further, though, it is crucial at this point to remember what that alternative is. *The alternative to minority demands for participation in public life is that the public square will be populated entirely by Christianity.* Minority demands for equal participation in public life might result in a secular public square or they might result in a religiously cacophonous one, but once a minority expresses its demand to participate, the decision as to which of these conditions will prevail is out of the hands of the minority and up to the will of the majority. So the baseline against which the decision about whether minorities should demand participation must be evaluated is a Christian public square. What I will argue here is that regardless of what the result of the minority's demand might be, either result (secular public square or religiously cacophonous one) is a lot (*lot!*) better than the alternative (a Christian public square).

As a side note, I feel like I should mention that I don't entirely know which end result I would prefer—a secular public square or a religiously cacophonous one. Over the course of writing this book and talking to people about it, I've considered the question quite a bit. Most people I've talked with who worry about there being too much Christianity in public life definitely prefer the secular public square result, and I agree that the benefits of that outcome are more clearly apparent and understandable than cacophony. Still, though, I remain intrigued and optimistic about the possibility of cacophony and think that it too would offer potentially substantial benefits, even compared to an entirely secular public square. Ultimately, however, since I'm sure that both results are preferable to a uniformly Christian public square, I've stopped worrying about the question. The answer is completely out of my hands, and nothing about my argument depends upon the answer, so I don't feel a need to argue that either result would be preferable to the other.

* * *

So, then, what are some of the possible advantages of a religiously cacophonous public square, as compared to an entirely Christian one? Here are four.

To begin with, pluralism and diversity are significant goods in themselves. The experience of public life is generally enriched by the presence of a variety of ideas, symbols, displays, traditions, clothing, music, and almost everything else. Such a public square is more colorful, more interesting, more stimulating, and more invigorating than one dominated by one belief system or culture, even if there may be important variations within that belief system or culture. A diverse and pluralistic public life is also more consistent with the best parts of our national history and identity, as enshrined in the free speech, free press, and free exercise of religion guarantees in our Constitution and exemplified by the many waves of immigration to America that have enriched our culture immeasurably over the past two hundred years. Of course, this is a personal preference, one that I hope most Americans share but that is quite obviously not embraced by everyone. If you prefer a version of America in which everyone is a white Christian, I don't really know what to say to you. I doubt I'd have any chance of convincing you otherwise, and I feel no need to expend my energy in trying. Enjoy Trump's America while it lasts.

Second, many minority groups and individuals will experience participation in public life alongside the Christian majority as an empowering exercise and fulfillment of the American ideal that the government should treat all people equally regardless of, among other things, religious belief or nonbelief. Of course, it is possible to enjoy the promise of equality without actually exercising it, but it is probably easy to understand why not everyone will be satisfied by, for example, Justice Kennedy's guarantee that anyone has the right to give an invocation before a town board if, in fact, everyone who actually gives one is a Christian. Active participation on equal terms—whether it be by giving an invocation before a legislature or receiving government money for a social services program inspired by one's beliefs or installing some type of symbol or display on public property— can provide those participants with a feeling of dignity, self-worth, and belonging that mere words may not.

Think here, for instance, of the reaction of the Wiccan community to its success in the Veteran Pentacle Quest. Wiccans still remember where they were when they heard about the victory, and one of the women who had applied to get a Pentacle on the headstones of both of her parents proclaimed, "I am ecstatic. It makes us equal in the eyes of the law again." Or consider the words of Keith Becher, one of the plaintiffs who sued Florida's Brevard County for refusing to allow Atheists to give invocations before the board of commissioners, following his victory in federal district court: "I am delighted the ruling favors equality. Atheists, non-believers, secular humanists and those from minority religions are an integral part of this community. We strive to be active participants and relish the opportunity to invoke the higher ideals that everyone in our community shares."

Third, an increased presence of minority belief (and nonbelief) systems in public life should result in a more educated and knowledgeable citizenry when it comes to religion and its alternatives. This is the most prominent theme that echoed through the words of the people I talked to while researching this book. Whether it's the Hindu American Foundation, which claims that engagement in the faith-based service process will "spread understanding of [Hinduism's] pluralistic and tolerant ideals," or the Muslim Interscholastic Tournament, which posits that the formation of Muslim Student Associations will "creat[e] an environment for . . . people of other faiths to become educated about Islam," or Selena Fox, who believes that the Pentacle Quest "succeeded in bringing about greater understanding about the Wiccan religion and Paganism, both in the USA and around the world," members of minority groups consistently say that participating in public life alongside

Christians has the potential to educate nonbelievers about their traditions and belief systems.

It is worth noting that this education can relate to one or more of at least three different aspects of religious tradition or belief. On the one hand, in some cases, it can inform nonmembers regarding the very *existence* of the tradition (and the extent of that existence), as in the case of the Summum, who were almost entirely unknown before they asked Pleasant Grove to put up a monument to their Seven Aphorisms. The education can alternatively, or additionally, concern the *content* of the belief system, as in the case of the Satanic Temple, whose beliefs are consistently misunderstood, even by those who are willing to stand up in public and denounce them. Finally, the education can relate to the *dispositions* of the believers, as illustrated by Nicole Niebler in her presentation at the Secular Student Alliance conference, who urged Atheists to go out and defy stereotypes by refusing to "argue about everything" and not showing "frustration if [religious believers] say 'bless you.'"

Giving invocations before legislatures and local boards may be the most effective way for minorities to contribute to this education effort. In a sense, a legislative invocation can serve as a mini lesson about the faith (or lack thereof) in front of an audience made up of local leaders and other engaged citizens. As David Williamson put it in chapter 3 when describing the importance of doing secular invocations: "I challenge anyone to tell me of a better time and place to get the message out about the secular values of inclusion, diversity, tolerance, and equality to the folks that need to hear it the most. When I or anyone else is doing an invocation, everyone at the meeting is standing at attention and is primed to conduct the business of the day." Or as Hindu leader Rajan Zed put it, invocations "create dialogue," which in turn "brings us mutual enrichment and assists us in vanquishing stereotypes and prejudices passed on to us from previous generations."

To be clear, I'm not suggesting that the American public—notoriously undereducated about religion—will suddenly become eligible for advanced degrees in religious studies as a result of the phenomenon I'm writing about here. There are a lot of reasons why many people, even when presented with factual information about this or that tradition or belief system, will remain no more educated than before. They may be willfully ignorant, or skeptical of everything they hear from people with whom they disagree, or so entrenched in communities whose members reinforce unsupported or discredited information that no amount of attempted education will make a difference. My suggestion is a more modest one—as minority participation in public life grows, we should expect to see at least some incremental increase in the understanding of minority religious beliefs (and nonbeliefs) among members of the general public.

Fourth, and finally, it is possible that when people become more educated and knowledgeable about religion, they will become more tolerant and respectful of those with whom they disagree. If this is correct, then minority participation in public life could in fact lead to greater social peace with respect to religion. Moreover, such social peace could extend beyond national borders, as more and more Americans gain insight and understanding into faiths that are more prevalent outside the United States. Admittedly, this is by far the most speculative reason to support the movement that I've described—whether a populace better educated about religion will be a more tolerant one is ultimately an empirical question that nobody knows the answer to for sure—but there are reasons to be optimistic.

For one thing, the relationship between understanding and tolerance makes intuitive sense. If intolerance and disrespect are rooted, as they often are, in a lack of understanding, then one would expect that a greater degree of understanding would result in more tolerance and respect. This is the position, anyway, of the United Nations Educational, Scientific and Cultural Organization (UNESCO), whose Web page states, "Laws are necessary but not sufficient for countering intolerance in individual attitudes. Intolerance is very often rooted in ignorance and fear: fear of the unknown, of the other, other cultures, nations, religions"; the Web page also urges lifelong engagement "to build tolerance through education."

Second, it is at least somewhat telling on the point that so many prominent members of minority groups, as related in this book, support minority participation in public life precisely because it may result in greater understanding of their beliefs. It seems unlikely that minority leaders would be pushing for something that would increase understanding and knowledge of their traditions if they thought that this understanding and knowledge would bring less rather than more respect and tolerance.

And finally, some limited studies have shown that, at least in the context of schooling, teaching *about* religions may in fact lead to more tolerance. The most prominent of these comes from Modesto, California, where researchers investigated the effects of teaching a world religions course on tolerance among the students in the course and concluded that "students taking the course showed statistically significant increases in passive tolerance, their willingness to refrain from discriminatory behavior, and active respect, the willingness to take action to counter discrimination." Obviously, studies like this one, focusing on teaching students in school rather than generally promoting education through participation of religious minorities in public life, hardly demonstrate that such participation will result in increased tolerance, but they do provide some support for the intuitive notion that the result is plausible.

* * *

A religiously cacophonous public square is not, however, without its dangers and difficulties. Here are a few, along with some thoughts about why they are insufficient to defeat the case I'm trying to make.

I will start with an observation. Throughout the book, I have more or less been lumping all minority belief systems together—Atheists alongside Muslims alongside Satanists alongside Hindus, etc.—as though these groups should consider themselves part of a unified and coherent movement. I've done this more for ease of discussion than anything else. Clearly not all members of all minority belief systems are going to feel comfortable being viewed as allies. Conservative Jews and Muslims, for example, are unlikely to see Atheists as compatriots, much less the Satanic Temple, and vice versa. I have no idea how Buddhists will feel being grouped with Scientologists. How are Taoist-Hindu relations doing these days? I don't know.

So I should clarify. Although it might certainly help the minority cause generally for groups with aligned interests to work together and look out for one another as they all seek to participate in public life alongside Christians, such concerted action is hardly necessary. Nothing I've said in the book requires that all minority groups agree with one another about their interests or even about the legitimacy of groups with whom they disagree. Muslims, for example, can and should continue to create Muslim Student Associations to take part in public life alongside Good News Clubs, even if they vehemently disagree that the Satanic Temple should be allowed to propagate its After School Satan clubs in classrooms next door. Atheists can and should continue to put up displays on public property during the December holiday season even if they don't look forward to seeing Jewish displays in the same area.

Similarly, by lumping all minority groups together, I have been concealing to some degree the fact that different groups and individuals, by the nature of their beliefs, will feel more or less strongly about wanting to participate in public life. Some may feel more wary than others about getting involved with the government. Some may not want to participate at all. As a result, even if my recommendations here were followed and resulted in religious cacophony, it would not necessarily be a cacophony that fully and truly represents the religious diversity of the country. Rather, it would be a cacophony skewed to some extent toward those groups that are more inclined than others to participate. The self-selection aspect of participation is an important point to recognize, but it's hardly an argument that those minorities who do want to participate should keep quiet. Even if not everyone participates to the same degree, a public square with greater minority participation will be one with greater diversity, pluralism, equality, mutual understanding, and potential for increased tolerance than one with less such participation.

This reasoning leads to a related third point, which is that participating in public life and becoming entangled with the government poses its own set of risks to those who do so. After all, one of the prominent lines of argument for separating church and state and insisting on a secular public square is that church-state entanglement can harm religion itself. For one thing, it exposes religious groups to public criticism, disparagement, and conflict, as they compete for resources, access, and approval on the public stage. We've seen countless examples of this dynamic throughout the book, although it's notable that most minorities seeking equal access to public life have persevered despite being attacked by Christian majorities and do not seem to have regretted it.

Additionally, reliance on government support can sap the energy from a tradition or make it vulnerable to manipulation by the state. For example, a religious school that becomes reliant on government voucher funding might find itself unable to resist changing its own mission if the government decides to place conditions on that funding. Imagine a voucher program, for instance, that changes its policy in midstream to require that all schools receiving funds must teach evolution—what, then, would a school founded on teaching the Bible as literal truth have to do? Either the school would refuse to teach evolution and lose what is probably a significant portion of its funding, or it would start teaching evolution, to the detriment of its own religious mission.

This too is a legitimate concern for minority groups that are considering participating in public life, although not nearly as large a concern as it is for the majority, since it seems improbable that a minority religious group in the United States would ever become overly dependent on government largesse. In any event, minority groups should certainly be careful, and they should pay attention to ensure that they are not being harmed in subtle ways by their increased participation in public life.

Finally, it is critical to recognize that once a public forum is open— whether it be for displays or invocations or public funding or public school access after classes are over—and minorities begin demanding participation in the forum, it is nearly impossible to use the nature or content of their beliefs as a basis for limiting who gets access to the forum. This legal rule leads to two related but somewhat different problems: on the one hand, the participation of parody groups and individuals, and on the other hand, the participation of groups that espouse beliefs antithetical to the ideals of our pluralistic, free, and equal society—the ideals, in other words, that are served by minority participation in public life in the first place.

By "parody groups and individuals" I am referring to those whose primary motivation is to protest the inclusion of any religion in public life by ridiculing religious beliefs and actions. I would put, for instance, Chaz Stephens—the guy we met in chapter 2 who puts up Festivus poles on government property—in this category. I would also at least tentatively include here the "Pastafarians," who believe in the Flying

Spaghetti Monster (FSM). As a federal district court in Nebraska concluded, after a careful and thoughtful analysis, the Church of the Flying Spaghetti Monster—which came into existence in response to the movement to teach "intelligent design" as an alternative to the "theory" of evolution in 2005—is "a work of satire, meant to entertain while making a pointed political statement."[†] Many people no doubt believe that the Satanic Temple is likewise a parody group, but it is not, at least not as I'm using the term. TST certainly employs parody as a tool in its campaigns, but that parody is only a fraction of what the Temple does, and it stems directly, as I understand TST beliefs (and to be clear, I am neither a Satanist nor a member of TST), from its theology of Satan as the ultimate rebel against arbitrary authority. TST, like most other groups that a majority of people would describe as "religious," engages in rituals, employs sacred texts, embraces a sophisticated theology, promotes a specific ethical creed, and is deeply rooted in a tradition that goes back centuries.[‡]

It is likely that if the movement for increased minority participation in public life continues, we will see more parody groups and individuals asking to join the fun. It may be possible for the government, in some cases, to manipulate the nature of whatever public forum it has opened up in a way that could exclude parody groups from participating, but that type of manipulation is fraught with constitutional difficulty and would likely face lawsuits, some of which would likely end up being

---

[†]   The case, Cavanaugh v. Bartlett, from the federal district court in Nebraska, was decided in April 2016. The primary thrust of the FSM, as I understand it, is that if, as intelligent design theorists proposed, the "intelligent designer" of the world cannot be identified specifically, then it is just as possible that the designer is a flying spaghetti monster as that it is anything else. Let me be clear--I adore the Church of the Flying Spaghetti Monster. Much of my early academic writing was about the "intelligent design" controversy, and like many critics of those who pushed for teaching that in the public schools, I welcomed the often hilarious antics of FSM. I base my tentative conclusion that it is a parody group on my reading of the FSM's public online materials, but I'm happy to be convinced otherwise if anyone feels like convincing me.

[‡]   On this point, I think it is instructive to read Doug Mesner's take on Chaz Stephens, whom Mesner criticizes as promoting a "sophomoric agenda." See Thomas Essel, *The Saga of Chaz Stephens, or How Not to Be an Activist*, on Patheos.com.

won. So, bet on more parody groups in public life. For some, this will obviously be a downside to the religious cacophony I've been defending; for these objectors, a true cacophony of sincere beliefs about the ultimate nature of reality might be acceptable, but one that includes ridicule and belittling of the beliefs of other people may go too far. Point taken. I'm on the fence about this myself. On the one hand, as someone who fashions himself a bit of a satirist, I think parody can be an effective and powerful way of engaging in public discourse. On the other hand, I recognize that many people hold religious beliefs very deeply and that those beliefs are the foundation of their entire existence. That's why I'm a strong proponent of free exercise rights of religious individuals and groups. I would hope that when minorities participate in public life, they focus on promoting their own substantive visions of what life means and how it should be lived, rather than on mocking opponents. But since there's probably no good way to constitutionally police this line, one can expect that some fraction of the increased minority contribution to public life that I'm supporting will likely take the form of tomfoolery, sometimes of a mean sort.

More problematic is the inevitable participation of individuals and groups who seek to promote views of the world that are contrary to the ideals of freedom, dignity, mutual understanding, and social peace that justify the inclusion of minority voices in public life in the first place. Some religious individuals and groups—think here of the despicable Westboro Baptists—ground their odious racist, sexist, or homophobic views in theological commitments. Of course, under the Supreme Court's current doctrine, these people can demand to be involved in American public life, as I've been using the phrase here, but if the movement to involve minorities in public life grows, as I've urged in this book, then it is probably likely that we will see such demands increase in the future.

Again, as with the parody situation, in some contexts the state might be able to manipulate the nature of its public forum to exclude such voices—notable here is the Supreme Court's ambiguous observation in *Marsh v. Chambers*, reiterated by Justice Kennedy in *Town of Greece v. Galloway*, that a legislative prayer practice may not disparage or denigrate other faiths§—but as in the parody context, this technique is unlikely to work most of the time. As such, the recommendations I'm making are likely to result in at least some increased involvement in public life by groups and individuals who assert positions that most people will find abhorrent and that run directly contrary to the whole point of having more minority involvement in public life to begin with.

So, how should we balance the potential advantages of increased minority participation in public life against the downsides—the potential harm to minorities themselves, as well as an increased potential for having to endure public expressions of both ridicule toward existing religious groups and racist/sexist/homophobic viewpoints? At the risk of being boringly repetitive, I will first restate my earlier point that it is quite possible, particularly if we do end up seeing a significant increase in hateful public speech, that government bodies will shut down their public forums altogether, resulting in a secular public square, which—for minorities anyway—would be preferable to a Christian one. But even if the result is cacophony, and even if that cacophony happens to include some hateful speech among all the rest, I think the benefits of public pluralism, equality, understanding, and possible long-term social peace are worth the risks. Given that we have seen few, if any, demands by such hateful groups and individuals to participate in public life thus far, it's unlikely that those demands will be plentiful in the future. In any event, though, the freedom to articulate unpopular ideas is one of the cornerstones of the First Amendment itself. The Supreme Court put it well back in its 1940 decision in *Cantwell v. Connecticut*, which invalidated the arrest of a Jehovah's Witness who played an album criticizing Catholicism on a public street, even though two men who heard the record wanted to punch him in the nose.

In the realm of religious faith, and in that of political belief, sharp differences arise. In both fields the tenets of one man may seem the rankest

---

§   It's always been unclear to me what this means. If Christian prayers before a legislative body repeatedly call for the "defeat of Satan," for instance, is that a disparagement of Satanism such that those Christian prayers can be (must be?) excluded? I don't know. My guess is that the Court doesn't know either.

error to his neighbor. To persuade others to his own point of view, the pleader, as we know, at times resorts to exaggeration, to vilification of men who have been, or are, prominent in church or state, and even to false statement. But the people of this nation have ordained, in the light of history, that, in spite of the probability of excesses and abuses, these liberties are, in the long view, essential to enlightened opinion and right conduct on the part of the citizens of a democracy. The essential characteristic of these liberties is that, under their shield, many types of life, character, opinion and belief can develop unmolested and unobstructed. Nowhere is this shield more necessary than in our own country, for a people composed of many races and of many creeds.

We are not quite at the point yet where our Christian majority is completely comfortable with the fact that we are indeed a nation of "many creeds," that we are indeed *not* a Christian nation. We've seen evidence of that from Pleasant Grove, Utah, to the Louisiana state legislature to Belle Plaine, Minnesota, and Little Rock, Arkansas, to the White House itself and beyond. I'm hopeful, though, that the minorities who have already started demanding their rightful place in American public life—Atheists, Satanists, Muslims, Hindus, Wiccans, and all the rest—will not be deterred, that they will persevere, that they will insist on being treated with dignity as equal members of society, and that, in time, they will be recognized as such. And when the day comes that some governmental body finally does give permission to the Satanic Temple to erect a monument on public property, and the citizens of the town have the courage to let it go up, I hope to be there to witness it. And I hope the day will be a peaceful one.

Acknowledgments

First and foremost, I would like to thank my wonderful editor, Emily-Jane Cohen at Stanford University Press, without whom this book would simply not exist. I would also like to thank members of the following audiences who listened to me talk about the book at different stages of its development and who offered terrific questions and comments that helped me improve the book significantly: the Boston University School of Law faculty workshop; the Boston University School of Law "Food with Faculty" program; the University of Minnesota Public Law Workshop (organized and led by the brilliant Jill Hasday); the American Constitution Society's Stanford Law School chapter; Americans United for Separation of Church and State's Rochester, New York, chapter, and the Satanic Temple national headquarters in Salem, Massachusetts.

In addition, I would like to thank the following individuals for their various contributions to the book: Stephanie Adams, Bernie Aua, Chalice Blythe, Adrienne Bossi, Elise Brown, David Ewing, Jeanet Ewing, Selena Fox (and her husband and assistant), Anne Fuzellier, Stewart Gollan, Todd Hirsch, Mussarut Jabeen, Richard Katskee, Shaza Khan, Jan McInroy, Su Menu, Doug Mesner, Maureen O'Rourke, William Reilich, Suhag Shukla, Nick Stancato, Kimber Starnes, Faith Wilson Stein, Linda Stephens, Katharine Stewart, Friederike Sundaram, Ron Temu, Fred Tung, Koren Walsh, David Williamson, and Rajan Zed.

Notes

INTRODUCTION

On the controversy in Belle Plaine, see Sandhya Somashekhar, "A Small Minnesota Town Is about to Get the Nation's First Public Satanic Temple Monument," www.washingtonpost.com, (May 6, 2017); Cory Zurowski, "Truce in Fight over Christian Soldier Image in Belle Plaine Park. Or Maybe Not," www.citypages.com (February 14, 2017). For a photo of the Satanic veterans monument, see Christopher Mele, "Satanic Temple Sponsors a Veterans Memorial in a Minnesota Town," www.nytimes.com (May 8, 2017). On the rally held by America Needs Fatima and the quote from Robert Ritchie, see Leonardo Blair, "Christians to Protest America's First Satanic Monument on Public Property," www.christianpost.com (July 13, 2017). Both Madison's *Memorial and Remonstrance* and Jefferson's letter to the Danbury Baptists can be found online at www.founders.archives.gov. Citations for the Court's anti-separationist decisions are as follows: *Good News Club v. Milford Central School District*, 533 U.S. 98 (2001); *Zelman v. Simmons-Harris*, 536 U.S. 639 (2002); *Van Orden v. Perry*, 547 U.S. 677 (2005); *Town of Greece v. Galloway*, 572 U.S. 565 (2014). On the 98 percent figure of colonists who were Christian, see Russell Shorto, "How Christian Were the Founders?," www.nytimes.com (February 11, 2010) (quoting Daniel L. Dreisbach). For Pew's 2007 and

2014 data on the demographics of religion in the United States, see Pew Research Center, *America's Changing Religious Landscape*, http://www .pewforum.org (May 12, 2015). For the more recent study on religious demographics in the United States from the Public Religion Research Institute, see its 2017 report titled *America's Changing Religious Identity* at https://www.prri.org/research/american-religious-landscape-christian -religiously-unaffiliated/. If you're interested in learning more generally about church/state law and the First Amendment, you can check out my first book, *Holy Hullabaloos: A Road Trip to the Battlegrounds of the Church/State Wars* (Boston: Beacon Press, 2009).

CHAPTER 1

Pretty much everything I know and have written about the Summum I learned from its fantastic website, www.summum.us, as well as the pamphlet *The First Encounter: A Never Ending Story*, which I received on my visit to the Summum pyramid. The U.S. Supreme Court case that held against the Summum is *Pleasant Grove City v. Summum*, 555 U.S. 460 (2009). The Utah Supreme Court case that held against the Summum is *Summum v. Pleasant Grove City*, 2015 Utah 31 (2015). The "Lemon" test comes from *Lemon v. Kurtzman*, 403 U.S. 602 (1971). The case involving the crèche in Pawtucket is *Lynch v. Donnelly*, 465 U.S. 668 (1984). The case involving the two separate displays is *County of Allegheny v. ACLU*, 492 U.S. 573 (1989). For the quote about how the endorsement test resembles interior decorating, see *American Jewish Congress v. City of Chicago*, 827 F.2d 120, 129 (7th Cir. 1987) (J. Easterbrook dissenting). Cites for the three Ten Commandments cases decided by the Supreme Court are as follows: *Stone v. Graham*, 449 U.S. 39 (1980); *McCreary County v. ACLU*, 545 U.S. 844 (2005); *Van Orden v. Perry*, 545 U.S. 677 (2005). Cites for the three Ten Commandments cases decided by the lower courts are as follows: *ACLU Nebraska Foundation v. City of Plattsmouth*, 419 F.3d 772 (8th Cir. 2005); *Felix v. City of Bloomfield*, 2016 WL 6634870 (10th Cir. 2016) [Westlaw cite]; *Card v. City of Everett*, 520 F.3d 1009 (9th Cir. 2008). The book about reaching sexual ecstasy is *Sexual Ecstasy from Ancient Wisdom* (Summum, 1993). If you want to buy yourself a nice big jar of Merh, you can start by going here (but keep those cats away): https://www.summum .us/merh.shtml.

CHAPTER 2

If you're interested in viewing the symbols that the Department of Veterans Affairs has approved for placement on the gravestones in national cemeteries, visit https://www.cem.va.gov/hmm/emblems.asp. The Adler book is Margot Adler, *Drawing Down the Moon: Witches, Druids, Goddess-Worshippers, and Other Pagans in America* (London: Penguin, 1979). The best sources regarding the history of the Pentacle Quest are those written by Selena Fox herself and published in *CIRCLE Magazine*, including "Nine Years of Disregard, Delay, & Discrimination by the VA," Issue 97, Summer 2006, 47–55; "Veteran Pentacle Quest Continues," Issue 98, Spring 2007; and "Success in the Veteran Pentacle Quest!," Issue 99, Fall 2007, 44–47. Fox's quotes about the Summum's being stuck in bureaucratic limbo and not being treated the same as other groups are from "Nine Years of Disregard," 53. The flag-burning case is *Texas v. Johnson*, 491 U.S. 397 (1989). The 2015 license plate case is *Walker v. Texas Division, Sons of Confederate Veterans*, 135 S.Ct. 2239 (2015). The case about the KKK cross in Columbus, Ohio, is *Capitol Square Review and Advisory Board v. Pinette*, 515 U.S. 753 (1995).

On the Atheist bench in Bradford County, Florida, see Associated Press, "Atheists Unveil Monument to Their Nonbelief in God," www .nydailynews.com (July 1, 2013); Olivia B. Waxman, "Unveiling America's First Public Monument to Atheism," www.time.com (June 28, 2013). On FFRF's atheist display in the Iowa courthouse, see William Petroski, "No-religion 'Nativity' Display Gets OK for Iowa Capitol," www.desmoinesregister.com (December 16, 2016). On the atheist display in Shelton, Connecticut, see Katie Toth, "Religion in the Town Square: Lawsuit Filed by Shelton Atheist," WSHU Public Radio, www.wshu .org (April 6, 2016). On the "Tree of Knowledge" in Lincoln, Nebraska, see Chris Bowling, "Atheist Capitol Display Unveiled without a Hitch," www.journalstar.com (December 19, 2015). On Chaz Stevens and his

Festivus poles, see Adam Manno, "Florida Activist Sets Up Anti-Trump Festivus Pole at Nativity Scene," www.orlandoweekly.com (December 2, 2016); Jessica Palombo, "Florida Man Airs Grievances with Festivus Pole in Capitol," www.npr.org (December 11, 2013). On the controversy in Leesburg, Virginia, see Caitlin Gibson, "In Leesburg, Holiday Displays Bring Controversy and Change," www.washingtonpost.com (December 16, 2011). On the Wiccan pentacle display in Green Bay, see Associated Press, "Wiccan Display at Green Bay City Hall Vandalized," www.winonadailynews.com (December 18, 2017).

Americans United's press release on the settlement of its pentacle lawsuit is "Bush Administration Agrees to Approve Wiccan Pentacle for Veteran Memorials," www.au.org (April 23, 2007). On Bob Barr's response to the Wiccan vernal equinox rituals at Fort Hood, see B. A. Robinson, Ontario Consultants on Religious Tolerance, *Conservative Christian Boycott of the U.S. Army*, www.religioustolerance.org (June 9, 1999; updated December 18, 2005). On President Bush's comments about Wicca, see Neela Banerjee, "Use of Wiccan Symbol on Veterans' Headstones Is Approved," www.nytimes.com (April 24, 2007). The *Washington Post* article quoting the woman who had applied for pentacles on her parents' headstones is Alan Cooperman, "Administration Yields on Wiccan Symbol," www.washingtonpost.com (April 24, 2007). Selena Fox's quotation about the legacy of the Pentacle Quest can be found in *Success in the Veteran Pentacle Quest!* (45). To learn a little bit more about the standoff between Selena Fox and Jeff Fenholt, see Associated Press, "Witch Claims Harassment," www.journaltimes.com (November 14, 1992).

CHAPTER 3

To listen to one version of Gary Gulman's hilarious riff on the Greeks, visit: https://www.youtube.com/watch?v=tfqccFBQeXk&list=PLpB_szg BShA6aJlR4ROgJ5uA5oi5s9uVI&index=36. The federal appeals decision striking down the Town of Greece's practice of starting its town board meetings with a prayer is *Galloway v. Town of Greece*, 681 F.3d 20 (2d Cir. 2012). The Supreme Court's decision upholding that practice is *Town of Greece v. Galloway*, 572 U.S. 565 (2014). The Court's first decision on the constitutionality of legislative prayer—the one that Justice

Burger wrote in less than five minutes—is *Marsh v. Chambers*, 463 U.S. 783 (1983). The case mentioned in a footnote about graduation prayer is *Lee v. Weisman*, 505 U.S. 577 (1992).

On Blake Kirk's invocation in Huntsville, Alabama, see Steve Doyle, "Wiccan Priest Opens Huntsville City Council Meeting with Prayer for 'a Spirit of Peace and Comity,'" www.al.com (November 6, 2014); Kay Campbell, "No Wiccan Priest for Huntsville City Council Prayer? 'Somebody Got the Collywobbles,'" www.al.com (June 26, 2014); Americans United for Separation of Church and State, press release, "The Wiccan Reads—and the City Survives: Diversity Comes to Huntsville," www.au.org (November 10, 2014). On Deborah Maynard's invocation in Iowa, see O. Kay Henderson, "Cabot Witch Delivered Opening Prayer in Iowa House Today," www.radioiowa.com (April 9, 2015); Jeff Guo, "What Happened When a Wiccan Witch Blessed Iowa Legislators," www.washingtonpost.com (April 10, 2015). On Nadim Koleilat's invocation in North Dakota, see Mike Nowatzki, "ND House Republicans Cancel Opening Prayer from Muslim on Ash Wednesday," www.inforum.com (February 19, 2015). On Duston Barto's invocation in North Carolina, see John Cominsky, "Chairman: Only Christian Prayers Welcome at Lincoln Co. Meetings," www.charlotteobserver.com (May 9, 2015); Adam Lawson, "Commissioners Create New Prayer Policy for Meetings," www.lincolntimesnews.com (August 4, 2015). On the hullabaloo surrounding a Muslim invocation in Delaware, see Matthew Albright, "Delaware Senator's Anti-Muslim Comments Draw Rebuke," www.delawareonline.com (April 5, 2017); Daniel Craig, "Delaware State Senators Walk Out of Session during Muslim Prayer," www.phillyvoice.com (April 6, 2017). On Rajan Zed's invocation in Idaho, see Betsy Z. Russell, "Idaho State Senator Defies Call for Apology to Hindus," www.spokesman.com (March 7, 2015); "North Idaho Senator Objects to Hindu Prayer," www.spokesman.com (March 2, 2015).

Americans United's "Operation Inclusion" can be found at www.au.org/content/operation-inclusion. The American Humanist Association's page on secular invocations is http://thehumanistsociety.org/invocations/. (The Humanist Society is an adjunct of the AHA.) Information on FFRF's "Nothing Fails like Prayer" competition can be found at https://ffrf.org

/outreach/nothing-fails-like-prayer. CFFC's terrific Web page about secular invocations both in Florida and elsewhere is http://cflfreethought.org/invocations/. On the controversial secular invocation in Lake Worth, Florida, see Michael Mayo, "Lake Worth Commissioners Walk Out on Atheist Invocation," www.sun-sentinel.com (December 9, 2014). On Aleta Ledendecker's secular invocation in Tennessee, see Bob Fowler, "Oak Ridge Council Members Boycott Secular Invocation," www.archive.knoxnews.com (January 12, 2016). On Athena Salman's secular invocation in Arizona, see Mary Jo Pitzl, "Arizona House Rules: Prayer Must Invoke a Higher Power," www.azcentral.com (April 19, 2017). On Thomas Waddell's attempted secular invocation in Maine, see Charles Eichacker, "Litchfield Man Cries Foul over Cancellation of 'Secular' Invocation for Maine Senate," www.centralmaine.com (May 29, 2017). On the secular invocation in Eustis, Florida, see Roxanne Brown, "Secular Invocation Sparks Controversy at Eustis Meeting," www.dailycommercial.com (May 8, 2017).

On Brevard County's "no atheists allowed" policy, see Dave Berman, "Brevard Sued over County Commission Invocation Policy," www.floridatoday.com (July 8, 2015). On the decision holding Brevard County's "no atheists allowed" policy unconstitutional, see Dave Berman and Wayne T. Price, "Federal Judge Says Brevard Not Allowing Atheists to Give Invocations Is Unconstitutional," www.floridatoday.com (October 2, 2017). The district court's decision in the case is *Williamson v. Brevard County*, 276 F.Supp. 3d 1260 (M.D. Fla. 2017). On the Pennsylvania House of Representatives' "no atheists allowed" policy and the lawsuit filed against it, see Nick Wing, "Atheists Sue Pennsylvania House after Being Barred from Giving Opening Invocations," www.huffingtonpost.com (August 25, 2016). The district court's decision in the case is *Fields v. Speaker of the Pennsylvania House of Representatives*, 2018 WL 4110560 (M.D. Penn. 2018) [Westlaw cite]. The district court decision rejecting Dan Barker's suit challenging the refusal of the U.S. House chaplain to allow Barker to give a secular invocation is *Barker v. Conroy*, 282 F.Supp. 3d 346 (D. D.C. 2017). The two cases coming out different ways on the question of whether legislators or town board members can give invocations themselves are *Lund v. Rowan County*, 863 F.3d 268 (4th Cir. 2017), and *Bormuth v. County of Jackson*, 870 F.3d 494 (6th Cir. 2017).

To view Dan Courtney's secular invocation before the Town of Greece board, go to http://cflfreethought.org/town-of-greece-ny-2014-jul-15. The online version of the article about my trip to Rochester is David Andreatta, "Humorist Finds Fodder in Greece," www.democratandchronicle.com (October 19, 2015). To learn more about pickleball, visit the U.S. Pickleball Association's "What Is Pickleball?" page at https://www.usapa.org/what-is-pickleball/. For Gregg Miesch's letter to the editor and related comments, see "Why Do Atheists Expend the Energy?," www.democratandchronicle.com (October 20, 2015). For Linda Stephens's comments to Heman Mehta, see "Town of Greece (NY), Center of Supreme Court Ruling, Will Have Two Atheists Delivering Invocations This Year," www.patheos.com (January 29, 2015).

CHAPTER 4

On the rally in Belle Plaine and the Left Hand Path's presence at the park on the same day, see Erin Adler, "Satanic Monument in Belle Plaine Prompts Weekend Rallies of Protest, Support," www.startribune.com (July 15, 2017). On the e-mails sent by opponents of the Satanic monument in Belle Plaine, see Evan Anderson and Lucien Greaves, "'Please Say NO to Satan' Emails Capture Minnesota City's Clash over a Proposed Satanic War Memorial," www.muckrock.com (August 21, 2017).

For books about the history of Satanism, see James R. Lewis and Jesper Aagaard Petersen, eds., *The Encyclopedic Sourcebook of Satanism* (Amherst, NY: Prometheus Books, 2008); Jesper Aagaard Petersen, ed., *Contemporary Religious Satanism: A Critical Anthology* (Farnham, Eng.: Ashgate, 2009); Per Faxneld and Jesper Aagaard Petersen, eds., *The Devil's Party: Satanism in Modernity* (New York: Oxford University Press, 2013); Asbjørn Dyrendal, James Lewis, and Jesper Aagaard Petersen, *The Invention of Satanism* (New York: Oxford University Press, 2016); Ruben Van Luijk, *Children of Lucifer: The Origins of Modern Satanism* (New York: Oxford University Press, 2016). On Romantic Satanism, see Peter A. Schock, *Romantic Satanism: Myth and the Historical Moment in Blake, Shelley, and Byron* (Basingstoke, UK: Palgrave Macmillan, 2003). On the Satanic Panic, see Jeffrey S. Victor, *Satanic Panic: The Creation of a Contemporary Legend* (Chicago: Open Court Publishing, 1993), and James T.

Richardson, Joel Best, and David G. Bromley, *The Satanism Scare* (New York: Aldine de Gruyter, 1984). The definitions of Satanism given by the two scholars are quoted from Mikael Hall, "'It Is Better to Believe in the Devil,'" in Faxneld and Petersen, *The Devil's Party*, 24. The two scholars, respectively, are Per Faxneld and Mikael Hall. The quotation about Satan in *Romantic Satanism* comes from Asbjørn Dyrendal, James R. Lewis, and Jesper Aagaard Petersen, *The Invention of Satanism* (New York: Oxford University Press, 2016), 30–31. The Church of Satan's Web page is www.churchofsatan.com. The quotation about Satanism's almost becoming extinct is from Amina Olander Lap, "Categorizing Modern Satanism," in Faxneld and Petersen, *The Devil's Party*, 84. The quotation about day care centers comes from Robert Hicks, *In Pursuit of Satan: The Police and the Occult* (Buffalo, NY: Prometheus Books, 1991), 182. The quotation about the dissipation of the Satanic Panic comes from Dyrendal, Lewis, and Petersen, *The Invention of Satanism*, 107. On the "Sinister Tradition," see Jacob C. Senholt, "Secret Identities in the Sinister Tradition," in Faxneld and Petersen, *The Devil's Party*, 250. The quotation from that article on despising ethical behavior is on 252. The estimate of the number of Satanists worldwide is from Faxneld and Petersen, introduction to *The Devil's Party*, 5. Lilith Starr's book is Lilith Starr, *The Happy Satanist: Finding Self-Empowerment* (Lilith Starr Studios, 2015). The website of the Satanic Temple is www.thesatanictemple.com. The article about TST's relationship with the LGBTQ community is Kate Ryan, "How the Satanic Temple Became a Queer Haven," www.vice.com (July 24, 2017).

On the Grand Junction invocation, see Erin McIntyre, "Satanist Gives Invocation Notable for Lack of Hellfire," www.dailysentinel.com (August 2, 2017). On the invocation in Pensacola, see Elizabeth Earl, "Satanic Assembly Invocation Sparks Protest, Possible Changes to Invocation," www.peninsulaclarion.com (August 18, 2016). On the one before the Kenai Peninsula Borough Assembly, see Jenny Neyman, "Kenai Assembly Hears Invocation from Satanic Temple," www.alaskapublic.org (August 15, 2016); Aaron Bolton, "Superior Judge Rules against Kenai Peninsula Borough in Invocation Case," www.alaskapublic.org (October 10, 2008). If you really want to watch the awful meeting of the Phoenix City Council, you can do so at www.youtube.com/watch?v=sC_ZIiL5zMg. For an article about the Phoenix situation, see Peter Holley, "How the Satanic Temple Forced Phoenix Lawmakers to Ban Public Prayer," www.washingtonpost. com (February 5, 2016). On the situation in Scottsdale, see Angel Mendoza, "Satanists Sue Scottsdale, Allege Religious Discrimination," www .azcentral.com (February 26, 2018). On the Boca Raton pentagram display, see Bethania Palma, "Pentagram Displayed at Florida Park Run Over by Angry Driver," www.snopes.com (December 20, 2016). On "Snaketivity," see Jonathan Oosting, "Satanic Temple Plans 'Snaketivity' Return in Response to Christian Nativity at Michigan Capitol," www.mlive.com (December 2, 2015). On Baphomet, see James Morgan, "Decoding the Symbols on Satan's Statue," www.bbc.com (August 1, 2015), and Leyland Devito, "Inside the Satanic Temple's Secret Baphomet Monument Unveiling," www.vice.com (July 25, 2015). On the controversy in Arkansas, see Andrew DeMillo, "Ten Commandments, Satanic Monuments Prompt Flurry of Calls," www.washingtonpost.com (September 11, 2016); David Koon, "'Do You Want a Baphomet Statue?'", www.arktimes.com (December 22, 2016). On the new monument in Little Rock and TST's plan to sue over it, see Benjamin Hardy, "Ten Commandments Rise Again at Capitol, but Satanic Temple Says Arkansas Law Is on Its Side," www .arktimes.com (April 27, 2018).

CHAPTER 5

On opposition by some Louisiana legislators to giving vouchers for use in Muslim schools, see Andrew J. Coulson, "State Rep. Balks at Voucher Funding for Muslim School," www.cato.org (June 15, 2012); Erin Gloria Ryan, "Republican Horrified to Discover that Christianity Is Not the Only Religion," www.jezebel.com (July 6, 2012); Gregory Kristof, "Louisiana Lawmakers Object to Funding Islamic School under New Voucher Program," www.huffingtonpost.com (June 13, 2012); Jarvis DeBerry, "Louisiana Lawmaker Needs Lesson in Religious Freedom," www.nola.com (*Times Picayune*) (July 8, 2012). On similar reactions in Tennessee, see Jonathan Turley, "Reading 'Riting and Religion: Tennessee Legislators Move to Kill Voucher Bill to Avoid Funds Going to Muslim School," www.jonathanturley.org (April 3, 2013); Jonathan Fagan, "Voucher Bill Could Fund Muslim Schools," www.murfreesboro-post.com (March 31, 2013); Andy Sher, "Tennessee School Voucher Bill Scrapes through House Committee by One Vote," www.timesfreepress .com (January 26, 2016). The lefty-leaning article about Mike Pence is Stephanie Mencimer, "Mike Pence's Voucher Program in Indiana Was a Windfall for Religious Schools," www.motherjones.com (December 2, 2016). The anti-voucher newsletter is *State Funded School Vouchers Support Teaching Hate for Kaffirs*, www.tn4politicaljustice.wordpress. com (March 27, 2016).

The citation for the *Everson* case is *Everson v. Board of Education*, 330 U.S. 1 (1947). The two key cases clarifying and simplifying the law concerning public aid to religion are *Mitchell v. Helms*, 530 U.S. 793 (2000), and Zelman v. Simmons-Harris, 536 U.S. 639 (2002). The case about the Missouri playground mentioned in the footnote is *Trinity Lutheran Church v. Comer*, 137 S.Ct. 2012 (2017). On the massive amount of money saved by religions because they don't pay taxes, see Dylan Matthews, "You Give Religions More than $825 Billion a Year," www.washingtonpost .com (August 22, 2013).

For Jim Towey's statement about Pagan faith-based groups, see Alan Cooperman, "White House Aide Angers Pagans," *Washington Post*, December 8, 2003; Simon Malloy, "Towey in 2003: 'Pagans' Neither Care for the Poor, nor Have 'Loving Hearts,'" www.mediamatters.org (August 24, 2009). For Pat Robertson's statement, see Wendy Kaminer, "Faith-Based Favoritism," www.prospect.org (December 19, 2001). On the Unification Church's receipt of federal funding, see Don Lattin, "Moonies Knee-Deep in Faith-Based Funds/Pushing Celibacy, Marriage Counseling under Bush Plan," www.sfgate.com (October 3, 2004). On the Church of Scientology's receipt of federal funding, see Rema Rahman, "Feds Fund Scientology-Backed Detox Program for Vets in Annapolis," www.capitalgazette.com (December 14, 2014); Brandy Zadrozny, "U.S. Pays for Scientology 'Experiment' on Sick Veterans," www.thedailybeast.com (August 12, 2015). On the Hare Krishnas' receipt of government funding, see Laurie Goodstein, "Bush's Call to Church Groups to Get Untraditional Replies," www .nytimes.com (February 20, 2001).

For an example of criticism of public funding of Islamic institutions, see Chuck Ross, "Mosque Linked to Muslim Brotherhood Has Received

Millions in Federal Grants," www.dailycaller.com (December 28, 2015). On Muslim institutions rejecting federal funds for "countering violent extremism," see Amy B. Wang, "Muslim Nonprofit Groups Are Rejecting Federal Funds because of Trump," www.washingtonpost.com (February 11, 2017); Safia Samee Ali, "Islamic School Walked Away from Nearly $1M in Federal Funding Because of Trump," www.nbcnews.com (March 6, 2017); Associated Press, "Fourth Muslim Group Rejects Federal Grant to Fight Extremism," www.foxnews.com (February 11, 2017). The website for the Islamic Schools League of America is www.theisla.org. For the *Huffington Post* study on voucher schools, see Rebecca Klein, "Voucher Schools Championed by Betsy DeVos Can Teach Whatever They Want. Turns Out They Teach Lies," *Huffington Post* (December 7, 2017).

You can learn more about the Al-Iman School in Raleigh at www .alimanschool.org. My account of the murders in Chapel Hill has been drawn from the following sources: Erik Ose, "*Why the Chapel Hill Shooting Was More Hate Crime than 'Parking Dispute,'*" www.huffingtonpost.com (February 18, 2015); Jonathan M. Katzmarch, "In Chapel Hill, Suspect's Rage Went beyond a Parking Dispute," www.nytimes.com (March 3, 2015); Margaret Talbot, "The Story of a Hate Crime: What Led to the Murder of Three Muslim Students in Chapel Hill?," www.newyorker.com (June 22, 2015); NPR Staff, "Chapel Hill Shooting Victims Were 'Radiant,' Teacher Says," www.npr.org (February 13, 2015); Sarah Kaplan, "'We're All One': Chapel Hill Shooting Victim's Heartbreaking StoryCorps Interview," www .washingtonpost.com (February 13, 2015); Jorge Valencia, "Razan and Yusor Abu-Salha Were All-American Sisters Who Loved Their Family, Service and the Beach," www.wunc.org (February 9, 2016); Moham-mad Abu-Salha and Farris Barakat, "Families of Chapel Hill Shooting Victims Speak Out on Anti-Muslim Hate," www.time.com (February 10, 2016); "Statement by the President," www.obamawhitehouse.archives .org (February 13, 2015).

For a brief summary of the Hindu American Foundation Guide, see "Hindu American Foundation Publishes Guide for Hindu Groups to Apply for Federal Grants," www.hafsite.org (September 2, 2005). The guide itself is Hindu American Foundation, *Faith-Based and Community Initiatives in the United States: A Guide for Hindu Organizations* (2005).

CHAPTER 6

On the controversy in Orange County, Florida, over the distribution of Bibles, Atheist literature, and the *Satanic Children's BIG BOOK of Activities*, see the following: Hemant Mehta, "Atheists in Florida Will Distribute Godless Literature in Local High Schools This Thursday," www.patheos.com (April 30, 2013); Leslie Postal, "Atheist Group Lawsuit against Orange County Schools Dismissed; Group Can Distribute Materials in High Schools," www.orlandosentinel.com (July 15, 2014); Lauren Roth, "Satanists Want to Give Out Materials in Orange Schools," www.orlandosentinel.com (September 16, 2014); Valerie Strauss, "Satanic Temple Challenges Policy Allowing Religious Materials to Be Distributed at Public Schools," www.washingtonpost.com (November 17, 2014); Doktor Zoom, "Satanic Temple's Fun Coloring Book Ruins Bible Handout Day in Florida," www.wonkette.com (January 15, 2015); Hemant Mehta, "After Satanists Planned to Give Away Coloring Books, Florida School Board Votes to End All Religious Distributions," www.patheos.com (February 10, 2015); "Satanic Coloring Book Prompts Fla. School to Ban All Religious Materials," www.talkingpointsmemo.com (February 11, 2015). You can buy the *BIG BOOK* at www.thesatanictemple.com/products/the-satanic-children-s-big-book-of-activities.

Katherine Stewart's book is *The Good News Club: The Christian Right's Stealth Assault on America's Children* (New York: PublicAffairs, 2012). The quotation from her book about targeting children is on 4. The unpopular school prayer cases are *Engel v. Vitale*, 370 U.S. 421 (1962), and *Abington School District v. Schempp*, 374 U.S. 203 (1963). The graduation case is *Lee v. Weisman*, 505 U.S. 577 (1992). The case about posting the Ten Commandments in schools is *Stone v. Graham*, 449 U.S. 30 (1980). The two evolution cases are *Epperson v. Arkansas*, 393 U.S. 97 (1968), and *Edwards v. Aguillard*, 482 U.S. 578 (1987). The after-school club cases are *Widmar v. Vincent*, 454 U.S. 263 (1981); *Lamb's Chapel v. Center Moriches Union Free School District*, 508 U.S. 384 (1993); and *Good News Club v. Milford Central School*, 533 U.S. 98 (2000). CEF's website is www.cefonline.com. The "728%" story is on 43 of Stewart's book. Stewart's quotes about Loyal Heights come from chapter 1 of her book, "The Good News Club Comes to Town," 9–36. The quotations about how public schools are "awash in religious literature," are from 99. The University of Virginia case mentioned in a footnote is *Rosenberger v. Rector and Visitors of University of Virginia*, 515 U.S. 819 (1995).

On distribution of Atheist materials in Delta County, Colorado, see Ryan Grenoble, "School District to Distribute Satanic Literature to Students on April 1," www.huffingtonpost.com (March 31, 2016); Colleen Slevin, Associated Press, "Satanic Book, Bible Sex Tracts Provided in Colorado Schools," www.coloradoan.com (April 2, 2016); Matt Kroschel, "Colorado School District: We Have No Choice but to Allow Atheist, Satanic Materials," www.denver.cbslocal.com (March 31, 2016). Stewart describes the events in Miami, Oklahoma, and Albemarle County, Virginia, on 99–100 of her *Good News Club* book. For more on Albemarle, see "Christians Won Court Case; Now Upset about Aftermath," www.patheos.com (June 14, 2007); Bob Unruh, "Pagan Christmas Ritual Pressed on Young Kids," www.wnd.com (December 8, 2006); Bob Unruh, "Teachers Rebel over Atheism Promotion," www.wnd.com (May 25, 2007); Americans United for Separation of Church and State, "VA. Pagans Advertise through Falwell-Secured School 'Backpack Mail,'" www.au.org (February 2007). The relevant Fourth Circuit case is *Child Evangelism Fellowship of Maryland v. Montgomery County Public Schools*, 457 F.3d 376 (4th Cir. 2006).

On Atheist after-school clubs, see Kimberly Winston, "Not Just Chess: Atheists Are Organizing High School Clubs, Too," www.washingtonpost.com (June 29, 2012). On the events at Pisgah High School, see Carol Kuruvilla, "N.C. School Reportedly Squashed Students' Hopes for Atheist Club," www.nydailynews.com (February 13, 2014); Hemant Mehta, "This Is the Real Reason an Atheist Club Isn't Forming at Pisgah High School," www.patheos.com (March 3, 2014). On the proposed Pagan club in Georgia, see Terence P. Ward, "Georgia Resident Pressured Not to Pursue Pagan After-School Club," www.wildhunt.org (November 14, 2017). The website of the Muslim Interscholastic Tournament is www.getmistified.squarespace.com. The page specifically about forming a high school Muslim Student Association is www.getmistified.squarespace.com/how-to-start-an-msa/. The website of the Secular Student Alliance is www.secularstudents.org. The page specifically about forming a high school secular student group is www.secularstudents.org/highschool.

TST's After School Satan website is www.afterschoolsatan.com. The creepy video with lots of spiders can be viewed at https://www.youtube .com/watch?v=b48-SBYbahQ. For more on the After School Satan program, see Katherine Stewart, "An After School Satan Club Could Be Coming to Your Kid's Elementary School," www.washingtonpost.com (July 30, 2016); Mary Bowerman, "'Educatin' with Satan': Satanic Temple Pushing After School Clubs," www.usatoday.com (August 1, 2016); Marva Hinton, "What's the Deal with the After-School Satan Club Movement?" www .blogs.edweek.org (October 21, 2016); Debbie Cafazzo, "After-School Satan Club Draws the Devout and the Curious to Tacoma School," www .thenewstribune.com (December 14, 2016); Jennifer Swann, "L.A.'s After School Satan Club Is Coming for Your Children," www.lamag.com (August 12, 2016); Cathy Free, "'After School Satan' Clubs Launch in Elementary Schools across U.S.," www.people.com (August 3, 2016) (quoting Doug Mesner); "Thousands Petition against 'After School Satan Club,'" www .cbn.com (November 11, 2016); "After-School Satan Club Fails in Tacoma District," www.cbn.com (September 19, 2017).

CONCLUSION

For Keith Becher's response to winning his lawsuit against Brevard County, see Central Florida Freethought Community, Press Release, www .cflfreethought.org (October 1, 2017). On public ignorance about religion, see Stephen Prothero, *Religious Literacy: What Every American Needs to Know—and Doesn't* (HarperOne, 2007). For UNESCO's view on education for tolerance, see http://www.unesco.org/new/en/social-and-human -sciences/themes/fight-against-discrimination/promoting-tolerance/. For the Modesto study, see Emile Lester and Patrick S. Roberts, "Learning about World Religions in Modesto, California: The Promise of Teaching Tolerance in Public Schools," *Politics and Religion* 4, no. 2 (2011): 264–88. For more about teaching about religion to promote tolerance, see Linda K. Wertheimer, *Faith Ed: Teaching about Religion in an Era of Intolerance* (Boston: Beacon Press, 2015); and Lauren Kerby, "Teaching for Tolerance: The Case for Religious Studies in American Public Schools," *Colgate Academic Review* 6, art. 7 (2012). For more about the Church of the Flying Spaghetti Monster, see the website at www.venganza.org. The case holding that FSM is a parody rather than a religion for purposes of the Religious Land Use and Institutionalized Persons Act is *Cavanaugh v. Bartelt*, 178 F.Supp.3d 819 (D. Neb. 2016). My most comprehensive academic article about intelligent design is Jay D. Wexler, "Darwin, Design, and Disestablishment: Teaching the Evolution Controversy in Public Schools," 56 *Vanderbilt Law Review* 751 (2003). For Doug Mesner's criticism of Chaz Stephens, see Thomas Essel, "The Saga of Chaz Stephens, or How Not to Be an Activist," www.patheos.com (January 12, 2016). The citation for *Cantwell v. Connecticut* is 310 U.S. 296 (1940).

Index

CPSIA information can be obtained
at www.ICGtesting.com
Printed in the USA
LVHW090058090519
617116LV00004B/105/P